Writings of the
Mystery of the Universes Book Two

Writings of the
Mystery of the Universes Book Two

by

Beverly J. Thompson

The Gathering Press

Writing of the
Mystery of the Universes – Book Two
by Beverly J. Thompson

Copyright © 2010 Beverly Thompson
ISBN 978-0-9794928-4-6
Published Summer 2010

Published by
The Gathering Press
Simpsonville, SC
www.thegatheringofangels.com

Contents of this book are copyrighted. No part may be reproduced by mechanical means, photocopy or computer without written authorization of the publisher (except for brief quotations by reviewers).

By reading this book, you, the reader, consent to bear sole responsibility for your own decisions to use or read any of this book's material. The Gathering Press and the author shall not be liable for any damages or costs of any type arising out of any action taken by you or others based upon reliance on any materials in this book.

To order more copies of this book, please visit the author's web site:
www.thegatheringofangels.com.

Interior design by Tony Stubbs, www.tjpublish.com
Cover artwork by Beverly J. Thompson and Sharon Free, Sharon Free Designs, www.thecreativediva.com
Photography by Madison Carter, www.honeymoonweddingphotography.com

Printed in the United States of America

Mystery of the Universes – Book Two   v

Contents

Dedication x
Acknowledgements xi
Foreword...xii
Introduction... xiv
About the Author.. xx

1 – Book of the Matrix...1
    The beginning of the second volume
2 – Book of the Charlatans...3
    Our creations as part of our game
3 – Book of the Nether 7
    Energy of the void by Nikola Tesla
4 – Read, Reread, and Reread 11
    All creation is the mind of the Creator
5 – Book of Temptations 14
    Move with your dreams
6 – The Road to Complete Sanity 16
    Each soul develops his or her own set of experiences
7 – The Force Field 20
    An individual's force field, The Lazarus Project
8 – The Means of Cooperation...25
    Cooperate with your self as well as with others
9 – Seek and Ye Shall Find..28
    What is it that you are looking for?
10 – The Turn of the Axis 30
    We are moving into a more realized system of
    co-genetic powers
11 – The Sands of Time 34
    The story of a boy and his dog opening to a new world
12 – Book of Generations 39
    The family that you call You is a part of the family
    of all living life that is termed God
13 – The Walk 43
    The return of You

14 – An Arm's Length Away 45
   You in the old world and the new world
15 – The Currents of Today..48
   Today, no yesterdays, no tomorrows
16 – An Encounter with Yourself...51
   You create your own movies
17 – Love in Action..54
   Mother Earth and Ultra-Humanity
18 – The Mother..57
   The new Earth
19 – Resurrection of the Mind, Body, and Spirit....................59
   Our planet and her inhabitants going back to their original forms
20 – The Unicorn..64
   The unicorn will come back in existence to bring a new dynamic to humanity
21 – Creation Within Creation Within Creation Within
   Creation 67
   Our process of ascension
22 – Founding Fathers...70
   Humanity is a composite of many extraterrestrial beings
23 – The Hearts of Morrow 73
   Perception
24 – A Clear Expression of You...76
   The Manchu Tribe who lived as a clear expression of their higher self as told by The Zealots
25 – The Mystery of Avalon 80
   Avalon is alive and well, this utopia being a choice
26 – Hear the Chalice of Your Words 83
   Reality – thoughts made manifest
27 – The Rise of the Roman Empire 85
   Earth's ruling party
28 – The Rumblings...90
   Some of the changes we will experience
29 – Cross Walks 93
   Our shifting evolution

30 – The Car Salesman 96
   A great metaphor about ourselves
31 – Trees in the Forest 101
   The microcosm in the macrocosm
32 – The Promise 104
   New seed of consciousness
33 – Now and Forever More 106
   Humanity shedding the costumes, Earth's power
34 – The Night Rider 108
   A template for the manifestation of visions into the newer dimensions of physicality
35 – The Chronicles 111
   Potentiality
36 – The Release 114
   This era of change, the Third Earth
37 – The Truth, the Tempest, the Witch 116
   A story about a small town
38 – Sodium 122
   An important substance for our bodies
39 – The Turn of the Century Into Biorhythms of Possibilities 125
   Each of you have built your very own matrix
40 – An Age of Understanding 132
   Crea, a new name for humanity
41 – The Time of Acceleration 134
   Change greater than we may think
42 – The Watch 136
   The plan devised by the heart of Earth
43 – Phase 1 Into Phase 2 139
   The angels speak of our huge transition
44 – The Solar Cross 142
   An advanced technological tool for voice and matter transmission
45 – A Tour of the Village Amanki 145
   A community of creator scientists
46 – The Condor and the Raven ....
   We are both

47 – The Round Table 152
    The truth of evolution – we set up this change
48 – The Art of Transformation 155
    Your outer world is only a projection of your inner world
49 – A Clear and Open Channel 158
    Thoughts, communication, and changing realities
50 – Basic Understanding of Breath 161
    The system called breath
51 – The Great Call 163
    The moving Earth and society
52 – The Focus of the Moon 166
    The center of earth's moon and how it affects us
53 – The Face of Tomorrow 173
    The spectacle about to take place is ready to meld into our plane of existence
54 – The Pump 178
    The Great Experiment project is over, onto the Grand Plan
55 – A Grass Roots Approach 185
    Our changing brains and the way we manifest
56 – The Uniqueness of You 188
    No two of us is exactly the same
57 – Shifting Sands Through Time 190
    You are the power to dream your dreams into reality
58 – The Mountain and the Molehill 193
    Opinions and judgements
59 – Focus 196
    What does "focus" really mean?
60 – Flying Colors 198
    The privilege of thinking for yourself
61 – The Importance of Art and Architecture 201
    Art, architecture, and music a reflection of inner life
62 – Finance 205
    Unity, a one world monetary system
63 – The Current 208
    The current that takes us to a new place of co-creation
64 – Blue Moon 211
    A new time line established

65 – Humanity 214
    The "horizon effect"
66 – The Impetus 217
    More on our future merkabas
67 – The Time of Remembrance 221
    The true deliverer of mankind
68 – The Works 224
    Trust in the power of You
69 – Lying in Wait 227
    The transformation of the pattern of creation
70 – Beyond the Material World of Temptations 231
    All shadows being illuminated
71 – From Whence We Shall Come 234
    Peace defined
72 – Foreverness 237
    Change in our perception of manifestation
73 – Artifacts 241
    Ancient artifacts and libraries being unearthed,
    information on and from Adolphus
74 – Recall 246
    A process, decisions to be made now
75 – Words 249
    Our changing communication through voice
76 – That Gut Feeling 252
    Our emotional center & changes taking place
77 – Abiding Peace 254
    Letting go of the ego's hold
78 – Your Circumstance 257
    Our current in transcending duality, A Conversation
    with Sananda
79 – The Magistrate 264
    Change in our perception of time
80 – Freedom 267
    Power and imagination
We Are One (poem) 270
Index 271

Dedication

To all humanity who chose to be here Now,
in this auspicious time of transition.

This very day, we know that we exist. We contemplate this existence. Yet we feel there is more. We are more than we could even imagine.

Awaken to the New World of endless possibilities.

We Are and Ever Shall Be. We are One.

Acknowledgements

A special thanks to my husband, Richard Thompson, who assisted me in understanding what was given in the writings. I have also shared some of these writings in our workshops and talks, and I truly appreciate everyone's input on this information. I thank all of you who have a hand in the new creations, bringing the higher dimensions of consciousness to the forefront. You all are to be applauded!

Foreword by Richard L. Thompson

We are all living in very interesting times. We are observing a major restructuring of our institutions and societal norms. These shifts are creating huge displacements for many, accompanied by anxieties and uncertainty. Many are openly opining that "I didn't sign up for this." However, in the larger picture, you did, indeed, sign up for this, the greatest evolutionary shift ever experienced by humanity as a whole. You, as a quantum being, chose to be here, now, to participate in the Shift of the Ages. Many wanted to experience what we are all living through, but we were chosen to be here, now, to facilitate these changes. No one can predict with certainty what these changes will look like in the future. We are creating it as we go. Nevertheless, we can say with certainty that it will be a world of individual choice and freedom, individual responsibility and consequence, in an environment of compassion, tolerance, and love.

The above are the true essence of our very beings. It is in our DNA. Although our third dimensional science has successfully mapped our physical genome, it still believes that our DNA is a double helix strand with "junk DNA" attached. However, we are so much more than that. We are quantum beings and "junk DNA" is connected to the quantum portion of us which is constantly messaging/communicating with our physical selves. As the greater frequencies of light (energy) reach our corporeal form from the universe, we are awakening to a greater portion of our true selves. We are and will discover that we have never been victims of anything, but instead the manifesters of the life we live.

This book, and its predecessor, gently and lovingly help us gain much insight into our greater beingness and what that means for us as we consciously embrace it. When you can open your mind and your heart, and feel the truth within, you will never be able to view existence in the same way ever again. It is a wonderful journey that is just beginning.

Introduction

"The new movement of mankind is his entrance into the Christ Consciousness. Man is becoming One with the Christ. It is a state of being. It is love incarnate." from "The Book of Temptations," a writing within this book.

The writings herein are a composite of eighty books explaining to us humans who we are and that is very powerful multi-dimensional beings. This is the second book of three (that is what I have been told) in the series "Mystery of the Universes." These writings are designed to assist in the opening of the human consciousness. Our life on this Earth has been an incredible adventure. These writings explain that we are our own creators, part of All That Is. Our world is rapidly changing, and these writings expand our awareness and knowledge to assist us to obtain wisdom, the wisdom of how and why we create in the third dimensional world now moving into the fourth and fifth dimensions of life. We chose this very life and continue to choose everything to create this reality. The process is amazing, and this book explains some of these processes.

Mystery of the Universes: a Prophecy Fulfilled, also known as the first book in this series, is a foundation of who we are as humanity, our symbiotic relationship with Lady Gaia, our Earth, our history on Earth, and our relationship with All. Most of the writings in the first book are ancient, brought forward to this time. Many of the writings are very esoteric and, admittingly, a difficult read, yet when studied, they give us such an understanding of the overall "mystery" of life, peeling off layers of our unconscious to reveal our very beautiful selves. Because every individual has his or her own perception, what they want to experience in each of their lives, each writing may deliver a slightly different message, depending upon each one's knowledge and wisdom base. These times of ascension were encoded in the human DNA, and these codes are now being activated. This series of books assist in this process. It is written where many of these writings can be found, although not in a very specific sort of way, but enough information is given where a true adventurer and explorer may be able to locate. I am hoping that many of these ancient writings will be found.

This Book 2 gives us a lot of information on our multi-dimensionality. This is repeated throughout the book, however, it is said or explained in different ways to help us understand this concept of who we are. The writings or chapters are called "books," each one independent of the other writings. However, there is flow helping us understand what is being said. We also are getting more than just a glimpse into how we will be creating and living in the higher dimensions, moving out of living in duality. We have been told life definitely will not be boring. We are experiencing and will continue to experience further earth changes as Lady Gaia, our Earth, gives birth to The New Earth, now overlaying the third dimensional Earth. This certainly is a very exciting time. We all chose to be here in this Now to experience this transitioning into the higher aspects of ourselves and The New Earth.

A basic understanding of the third dimension (the dimension this Earth and humanity has resided in for millions of years) is that all life is physical not knowing that we all are spiritual beings. As spiritual beings, we incarnated into this physical reality (we planned it) doing our part of Creator to more fully understand just what it means to be a creator. So the veil was put into place so we could play out our plan. The fourth dimension is a transitional dimension, a doorway into the fifth layer of consciousness. It is the beginning of understanding love and Oneness. The fifth dimension is manifesting through our heart/mind, living in Oneness, a higher understanding of the process of creation coming through our part of Creator known as our Higher Self. This all is further explained in this book. These writings are to let you know and remember this plan we all as One put into place. Are you having fun yet? As you begin to truly understand this wonderful dimensional shift you will know what you signed up for and love it for what it is.

All of the books were written through the process of interdimensional communication, also called channeling or hypercommunication – having a conversation with other beings or our Higher Self across dimensional lines. This gives us access to information outside one's knowledge base. We all have this ability within us, although some people are more adept at using this part of themselves. As each of us moves further into the higher dimensions, we will experience more of this communication. In the churches, it is known as having a "mystical" experience. It is called mystical because it is not understood. Those who wish to stay in the third dimension have that option to continue experiencing duality. Within Creator, there is no judgement, better than or less than, only whatever a soul wishes to experience. All of us are part of Creator Source and are deeply loved.

I use a lot of discernment in what I read, hear, and channel. I laugh at myself when I question something I receive in my communications that doesn't seem so far out, yet totally accept information that appears to many so far out there, even though we are told there is no out there out there. As we are learning, our world is a projection of our thoughts. We create our own reality through these thoughts. When I feel that truth is spoken, I know it. And this "feeling" is the difference. You, the reader, always use your own discernment. Do not worry if you don't understand what the writing is saying. As each one of us progresses, many of the writings take on an added meaning and understanding. What we at first did not understand may become perfectly clear as we move up the ascension ladder. In many of the writings I have added questions and they, my inter-dimensional friends and Higher Self, have answered to help clarify what was communicated, some answers given me while putting this book together. Many of the names in these writings may be different than those in our history or other people's channelings. I spelled them as I "saw" them or as close to how I "heard" them.

The first writing in this book was written on September 11, 2006, while I was compiling the information on my first book. The last writing called "Freedom" is dated April 12, 2010. The non-bold italicized words are my own. We are changing so rapidly and many of the changes are being felt and seen. As an intuitive counselor, I have been witness to many messages and visions of an advanced world. I have seen changes in our technologies, a change in perception of some of our mental disorders (they aren't disorders after all), more integration of the elemental kingdom (fairies, devas, etc.) and their assistance with our plant kingdom, finance and our world monetary system, healthcare, and so on. For ongoing messages and articles from me, my husband, Rick, and other wonderful lightworkers, see our website, www.thegatheringofangels.com. I feel we definitely have been transitioning for many years and this will continue. This third dimensional duality program is coming to a close. Breathe in the New World. We are in for a big ride, get yourselves ready and let's go!

One of my messages explains a simple view of ourselves, and I wish to share it here.

The Story

You and Earth are a story in the making. Many of your myths were centered around astrological events that have taken place and had an affect on you and the planet. This story that is being developed is your story making his-story or history. As you change your perceptions, your story changes also and you see your history in a whole new way of understanding. As your story develops, your characters change. Some of the characters change their names, sometimes their gender as they are here on this earth plane for a reason. They may come here to challenge themselves with new creations, creations not known on their home planets. They may come here to develop a new scientific method, working to understand the quantum physics of the world they embodied in. They may come here to enhance their emotional body, a body that is a more unique part of the human (God in man). They may return to Earth as many times as necessary to bring about the changes they so desire within themselves. It is such a mixture of stories, each individual part of Creator experimenting life biologically, emotionally, and mentally all wrapped together as Spirit having a human experience. This plan each one of you have devised is really very grandiose. You decided to separate yourselves from another part of you (even though that really is impossible), and the plan has worked. Most of you have forgotten that you are a part of something bigger, and you have termed this "bigger" God. Many say: "God is in charge of my life. I hand it over to him." To be gender correct, you can now say himher since "God" is both female and male – you!

Your world is now thinking what kind of plan would God devise with all of the chaos that is going on in this world. How would He bring us all together? The Christian community says that the Second Coming is at hand. And it is, but Jesus will not return on a cloud to save anybody because there is no need to save anybody. Each of you has incarnated as both female and male, many anybodies. There is no anybody to save. How can that be when you have incarnated as human, not counting your non-human bodies, many times? What you will soon be seeing are the many religious communities starting to understand this process of incarnation. They will start seeing themselves as many instead of just one. This sets up a whole new look at life and how it has evolved. Snippets of past lives will be coming into view for many people. At first, it will be difficult to understand what is going on, but they will soon realize themselves playing various roles. Their stories will then become multi-faceted.

What a story you all have developed. It is indeed, very interesting. Each one of you has so many novels you have dreamed and experienced. And so it continues on, adding more chapters to this ever-evolving mystery of being human. Splendid work indeed!

In peace, gratitude, and love, many blessings to Us All.

About the Author

Beverly was born in Fort Wayne, Indiana, and she and her husband now live in upstate South Carolina, as do her three children. Beverly became interested in metaphysics at a young age, then started studying the issue of consciousness and the paranormal in the 1980s. In 1998, she started communicating with the Ascended Masters, particularly Sananda, who assisted her with opening up to a whole new world of form and thought. Through the Masters and other channels, she has had numerous and ongoing so-called mystical experiences (but not so mystical when we understand our multi-dimensionality), visions, and conversations through the dimensional veils. Beverly's intuitive counseling skills have brought her to an even keener understanding of a soul's choices, knowing that each soul's incarnation into a human body creates his or her own experiences in order for them to grow in their understandings and wisdom. Besides being an author and intuitive counselor, Beverly is an ordained minister, spiritual teacher, speaker, and energy therapist. She also has worked in the area of interior design for many years, feeling one's home or business should support one's work or lifestyle, a sanctuary to excel, reflect, and feel comfortable in.

Beverly and her husband, Rick, who also communicates inter-dimensionally, writes and speaks, publish a quarterly newsletter and their website, www.thegatheringofangels.com.

Metaphysics: systematic study of the science of Being, transcending the physical. A branch of philosophy and science, metaphysics is concerned with "who are we?" and "what is our place within creation?" It is the science or theory of knowledge of the most speculative or esoteric nature. A phrase taken from the first book, *Mystery of the Universes:* "You are divine. You can be no less." This present age is known as "The Age of Science of the Divine."

September 11, 2006

Book of the Matrix

This is the beginning of the second book or volume of what appears to be a mystery. No longer will these thoughts and knowledge be a mystery with the understandings that are being given within the texts of these books. You have succeeded in making these mysteries (knowledge) available to the masses so they can move to their appointed time and place.

Mankind, remove all of your blinders that you have placed over your eyes and ears. Hear Spirit God within and move forward into the complete knowingness of yourselves.

This matrix that you have built for yourselves is being opened for you to see, hear, and know yourselves and recognize what this great Mother Earth, Gaia, has done for you, humanity. Also, each of you will begin to see yourselves differently, as a part of the One God. You will begin to recognize the various star systems from whence each of you have come. You will recognize your brothers and sisters of the stars. You will be able to travel the skies and once again meet with those brothers and sisters that you have been most close to.

You have served well and are being served by the holy love of Creator. We impart this knowledge for you to comprehend what you have built for yourselves and all of God/Creator.

We are the divine beings, just as each of you are, who have come to serve humanity in this great change. I Am Sananda, I Am Archangel Uriel, I Am Archangel Michael, I Am Thoth/ Hermes, I Am within the great Order of Melchizidek. We are and ever shall Be.

January 10, 2007

Book of the Charlatans

There was a time when mankind was stirring in their skins and felt they were a part of something greater than their bodies. They felt an imbalance. They moaned and groaned until the day of reckoning. They awakened from their slumbers. They sighed with relief that they now knew their origins. Mankind, you again are going through this process. Does this process need to be repeated? It is up to each and every one of you.

This book is located in the caves under your seas. The fragments of these books will emerge with the turnings of your waters.

You, the maker of heaven and the earth. What is the process? What has come of this process? What is the reason for this process? Man, created as man and woman, why? We, who perceive our bodies, are the containers of our souls. What are we containing? Answer our prayers, answer our questions. What have we done to continue on this adventure of being in the flesh? You who we guide our questions to, who are you? What will come to pass when we know this information? In the ruins of the temples that have been built in areas on this orb, why are they placed where they are? What makes them tell the time? We have many questions. Will they be answered?

In our slumber we awaken to another world. Sometimes this world looks very familiar. Other times no one and nothing is familiar to our eyes, hearts and minds. Yet in our visions, it all is familiar. Which is our real world?

We have many questions that we want answered. Would you please communicate with us so we have a fuller understanding of who we are?

My dear Brethren,

Why do you ask so many questions when you already have all the answers within you? Do not turn and look at your fellow man for answers. Just stop and look right into yourselves. We are not asking you to look into your physical body as such even though the physical body supports the real you. We are asking you to look beyond the physical which is you, the energy of you. Beliefs in the afterlife is a way for you to understand that you are more. You have created this game of the physical. We call it a game because it isn't really you. Yes, it is a part of you but not the all of you.

In the temples you will find that a heaven exists, a very peaceful heaven. Heaven is not somewhere out there but inside your very own selves. Yet you have built yourselves beautiful temple buildings and have placed them at certain points on the earth that you stand on. You have felt impulses at these areas. You have felt life pulsing at these areas. You have felt an internal peace in these areas. So you ask, why is that?

Within your selves you know that this energy, the impulses of this earth are a part of yourselves. You feel a closeness to the ground on which you stand. Go back into your temples and stay there until you find that inner peace and love that you will understand. You will understand what you have built for yourselves. You will know that you have built a control system yet you give yourselves free will. Remove your masks and take a look at You. You have built this plane of existence and have monitored it since its inception. This collective energy is a base for the collision of mutated energies from various aspects of yourself. When you tire of your games, you will absolutely understand and know what game you have presented yourself. You may leave your game at any time or continue playing until you decide that you have had enough. Then you can say it is over and return your consciousness to the All of You.

What you have done in this time and place is project out your thoughts, dreams, and desires, therefore you have full control of your own projections. If you wish to continue, then you can move your projections anywhere and anytime. Then you will know that time and place are part of your projections. You have built quite an amazing universe and many more universes are being developed. This is your game and you are in total control.

I Am the Collective You.

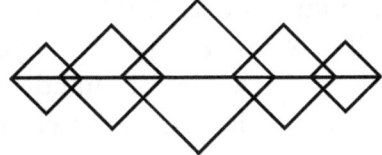

Q - These awakening periods, how many have we had on this earth plane?
A - Since there is no time and place, you have continued playing the games. However, you have changed your games many times in your part of this universe. When you see the other universe you have projected, you change your game. This time period you call the new millennium is one such time. Most changes will take place within the next seven years. *(Please note this writing is dated January 2007).*

Q – You said when we see the other universe we have projected. Please explain.

A – You live in more than one universe (dimension) simultaneously. You have yet to fully perceive this, but you are now making changes to allow this perception into your consciousness. Perhaps this shall be written "other universes," yet all is contained within the One (Omniverse).

Q – *The definition of "charlatan" according to the dictionary is "one who pretends to more knowledge or skill than he possesses; a pretentious imposter". Please explain the title of this book.*
A – Look at the word imposter. These lives that we live in the physical is such a small part of who we really are and is not the total of our existence, yet many have believed it so. Therefore man has created himself as an imposter of who he truly is. The game is changing. You are coming out of your slumber, wiping the sleep from your eyes and seeing the world (and worlds) in a very different way.

My most beautiful ones, see the life that is you. It is beyond the physical, well beyond the physical that you are experiencing. Open your eyes that are in your minds and you will see a vastly different world. Be in peace, be in peace.

January 16, 2007

Book of the Nether

This book describes what is called the nether. The nether is energy in its purest form in that it is formless. The scientists that have come up with this information have lived on this planet as well as other major star systems to help themselves understand physical creation. They lived on your planet in many incarnations. Tesla was one such scientist. Telsa's work is being studied in great detail today.

— *Nikola Tesla 1857 – 1943*

The inventions of man and other planetary beings who have studied the energetics of the universe have found that energy in its purest form is static. It moves with the force of thought which in itself is an energy. However, the thought is created energy that has been arranged by the frequencies of the One.

When it became known that the teutonics of the frequencies reached a vibration of 120 megahertz, the nether arranged itself as the force (thought) was sent out. To send out is a misnomer as there is no thing out there. All energy resides in the void of existence. However as beings perceive this energy, they perceive as separate the various created energies or creations. To take this a step further, the One mind encompasses all creation so there is no thing outside of itself. With the thought of separation as a means to extend out from the created One, then all creations are the projections of One creation.

To further move back into this One mind, all thoughts inside the One shall project into the energy of which it is. This spark of light continues on inside of itself but is viewed by beings as the cosmos. This cosmos has taken on many forms. Another way of saying this is the cosmos is made up of many variations of the nether.

The study of this phenomena will be as a break through of all forms of energy including all types of electrical power and stimuli, aerospace, and aerodynamics. What is seemingly out of control of most beings, in this case humans, is not out of reach or control. Since we are all a part of the One mind, then we can project "out" to form any creation that we want. We have all the tools within us and within our grasp.

This book is a forerunner to the sciences of the ages. When man knows he has all capabilities of the arrangement of nether, then anything and all things can be changed with the blink of an eye. And in order for creation to work for the betterment of the One, all false thoughts of power control must be dropped or transmuted so the new possibilities of grand creations can be entertained.

The earth is changing to another form. What has been the norm for the various types of energy configurations will no longer be valid in the new earth. I have had the privilege of seeing into the future with my mind control. Many of my experiments that have not worked in this day will be as the new science when the earth is ready for the change.

Take a look at the rotator engine that runs on sparks of electricity that pulse at two rates. This has created a movement. In the future when this earth vibrates at another frequency, then this same engine will be powered by the pulsing of three electromagnetic waves that intertwine to create a smooth movement which will enable machines to ride on air with very little sound.

This recording shall be released at the time of change. It

shall be used in the strictest of confidence by those people who work for the love of life. Any thoughts of control over another, the technology will not work because the mind of the scientist has to be in accordance with the love of the One, or be in accordance with the proper movement of the nether.

I have lived many lives and continue my research on many levels of creation. On the earth I was known as Nikola Tesla.

This writing is about quantum physics. Our understandings of the Universe(s) are changing as we recognize that our physics change when we move into other dimensions. Long after receiving this writing, I came across information from one of my favorite group entities, Kryon, channeled through Lee Carroll (see www.kryon. com). In Kryon's message dated February 14, 2010, titled "Needed Science for the Times," it explains the future of science. Kryon says it's possible to alter the mass of objects, therefore the affect gravity has on them changes. He goes on to say that there is no such thing as anti-gravity, only the control of mass (atomic density). This all has to do with magnetics. Tesla experimented with magnetic fields, and he said in this writing that when earth vibrates at another (higher) frequency, we will have machines riding on air.

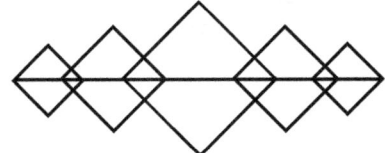

Q – What is meant by "teutonics of the frequencies"?
A – The word "teutonics" means movement, base word "teu" – to release, and "tonic" – pertaining to a tone.

Q – I have read through my research in the Internet (see Wikipedia) that the megahertz is a unit of electromagnetic (EM) wave frequency equal to one million hertz. The unit is occasionally used *in measurements of bandwidth for high-speed digital data, analog and digital video signals. An EM signal of 100 megahertz is near the middle of the standard frequency-modulation (FM) radio broadcast band, and has a wavelength of 3 meters, which is a little less than ten feet. This writing says that the teutonics (a release pertaining to a tone) of the frequencies reaches a vibration of 120 megahertz, the nether arranges itself as the thought is sent out. My comment is that seems to be a low frequency. Any comments?*

A – As you are learning, thoughts become things. The human has incredible capabilities within the heart/mind. Your thoughts, indeed, create your reality. You each are much like your own radio station. Your thoughts project out and affect your reality. The higher your frequency, the further your thoughts are projected, and the more they work for you and touch another (when and if they allow). Unconditional love for all is the highest vibration the physical can enjoy. When you live in such love, including love of self, miracles (or seeming miracles) abound.

Q – Has Nikola Tesla lived any other lifetimes on this earth that we may be familiar with?
A – He has lived one life that is remembered by the name of Artemis. (see *Writings of the Mystery of the Universes, Book of Nature*).

March 15, 2007

Read, Reread, and Reread

It was once said that all creation is the mind of the Creator. And they were right! Yet they did not realize that they were/are the creators. What is it in man that refuses to understand his true existence? Perhaps that is why man needs "proof" of his existence.

Man, born of the Father, begotten of all Creation, read these words to comprehend your existence. Know that your body is you but not the all of you. Know that the all of you is part of another All. And know that the All encompasses All Creation. And know, that all Creation is the All, now and forever more.

Release the need to know the All. Just know that you are to do your part in the All. Religions, a multitude of theologies have sprung up on many planes of existence, and many of them have come to this earthly body. They have brought with them their interpretations of what is. They have brought with them their ideologies, their sciences, and their need to understand the All. No human, past, present, or future, will totally comprehend the All. It is so vast, so complete, so loving. It is beyond the beyond the beyond. Just know that life IS and that you will forever BE.

Now, what is your purpose? You, as it has been said, are the maker of heaven and earth. Heaven is not a place but a state of being. This earthly plane is going back to its roots. Its creation is to bring into alignment the forces (energies) of the Godhead. The Godhead is each of you in your entirety, each a part of the All. Your being the Godheads are making the new creations out of your heaven on this earth. Not only is this earth being affected, but the other planets and solar systems, and galaxies are being affected since you each are part of the All.

You may sense your beginnings, a most difficult thing to do. How can you know that you burst into being? No, it was not when you were birthed as a baby in this lifetime, but you were birthed into existence at the birth of All That Is. Now, how can that be? All life was, is, and shall be.

Think of life as the following. Breathe deeply into your beingness and you will eventually see "nothing or no thing". That no thing is you, all of you, a part of the All. Yet, you see yourselves as something or some thing! Every breath that you take, you breathe in the prana of life. You are that prana. You are the arrangement of prana. In an earlier "book", the prana was called the nether *(see Book 3 "Book of the Nether")*. It is the same. How does prana become prana?

To truly comprehend that last statement is not possible, at least not in your human forms. As was stated earlier, there is no need to understand completely, because you are still creating your completions. Life is infinite. Your creations become complete. You, as your own Godhead, have always been complete. Therefore, you are always creating. You are always creating movement of energy or prana. You are always and create in all ways. You have been given these abilities by the god internal and the god eternal. You are not a mistake. There is no such thing as a mistake. It is only the process of creating that may be determined to be a mistake. But that can never be, because all creation is a process. There is no right, and there is no wrong. It just is creation.

This movement of creation is changing for you, the collective All. It is changing because you have created it so. You All are moving into a new time and new place of understanding. You are creating new movements, doing it differently. Therefore there are great changes being made in all of creation.

There are continued bursts of energies, of creations, continually creating. The edge of this universe continues into the next universe (set of frequencies), and that universe continues into the next. It is never ending, always expanding. Each of you is an intricate part of the All. Know that you Are and Ever Shall Be.

We stand as One. We walk as One. We talk as One. We create as One. We are One. Any one, any thing is One. We move as One. We balance as One. We understand as One. Yet we have divided our One so that we grow as One. We contemplate as One. We Are and Ever Shall Be.

This very day, we know that we exist. We contemplate this existence. Yet we feel there is more. We are more than we could even imagine. We are One, we are One.

May 1, 2007

Book of Temptations

In these times and this very moment, all is as it should be because it cannot be anything else. Many of you were brought up by family members involved in the church. You may have studied the word temptation. What does this word really mean? In this book, we shall look at this word from another perspective.

The thought forms of man continue on until the day that man thinketh not. How can man thinketh not? Man is a thinking machine, is he not? That is what he was designed to be, a thinking co-creator, thoughts being manifested through the vessel of physicality. Yet man is so much more than that.

Remember the days as a child sitting and watching the stars at night, the leaves and grass with the early morning dew upon every blade, and the birds and insects in flight looking for whatever they want. You may have thought, "What freedom they have. They can fly anywhere just with the flap of their wings."

Mankind, you can do the same things and even more with just your thoughts. You are a most magnificent machine of such great powers. You have surrendered to an omnipotent God/Goddess, the love that you hold within and the love that you exert through your bodies. You have the ability to fly anywhere and anytime. Now is the moment that you take the truth into your being and magnetize the most wondrous thoughts of creating an even more magnificent universe. This universe shall be comprised of love manifested through your magical thoughts. These thoughts are dreams made with love. These thoughts are your hearts desires made manifest. These thoughts are your feelings made manifest. These thoughts are your finest choices made manifest upon this earthen plane.

What do you suppose brought on these desires of the body, mind, and spirit? You are an infinite god made manifest by your own very selves. What once was (and still is) called a simple temptation is a dream. What you once felt was beyond your capabilities, you can now manifest in this holy time. The truth of the parable of Adam and Eve is the taking of the fruit of knowledge, manifesting the knowledge of what you are! The fruit or knowledge is always there for you to grasp. The old stories of temptations as something "bad or evil" will come to an end. They are no longer needed as you, mankind, moves into this wondrous state of love incarnate.

Therefore, the word "temptation" is just a word that means move with your dreams. The new movement of mankind is his entrance into the Christ Consciousness. Man is becoming One with the Christ. It is a state of being. It is love incarnate. Dream mankind, that this holy time is your entrance into the Kingdom of Heaven while in your physical bodies. Yes, you will maintain your physical bodies if you so choose. Life is always your choice.

This book is written by the collective you. It is written in your hearts and you will understand its truth because you (all of man) wrote it! This movement toward Christ Consciousness was written in the Records, therefore in your very own DNA.

May 18, 2007

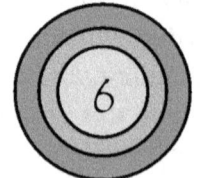

The Road to Complete Sanity

The forces of these times are in adherence to the mass consciousness. Each human on this earth plane has developed his or her own battery of new found experiences. This book deals with some of these experiences and what each has placed in his or her own path to achieve their intent. Namaste.
Who are you?
  Guardians of those paths.
  Greetings in the name of the One. We are here to discuss what you have laid out before you for you to continue your sojourn to a more balanced you. Each one of you has your very own story and no two stories are exactly the same. In fact, they are all quite different! Be assured that no two paths will converge and wipe out your path or the other's. That is not possible.
  To begin on one's sojourn, each one of you has placed the veil around you to hold out any interference of past or future lives. You are to concentrate on just this one life. You may get snippets of your other lives that may assist you in this life. That, indeed, is very healthy. Many of you have read the book, "You Are Becoming a Galactic Human"[1]. Well folks, you already are a galactic human. You exist in many realities, dimensions, and

places of existence. Sound confusing? Each of you dear humans has chosen to be here now at this time and at this place. You have chosen it for the mere fact that you want to grow within yourself. Your growth is your bargaining chip to reach into another space and time. This bargaining chip is not given by anyone other than yourself. You have decreed it so! By becoming human, you will have surpassed all ways of creator creating. You are the new way. You are the leader and you will continue on leading. Those forces "out there," your guides and angels, continue on the path with you. Can you understand the enormity of this whole "process"?

You have begun a process where you create from your heart-mind. You use your solar plexus to bring in information that is either digested or discarded, whatever is for your personal highest good. You may retrieve information that you have stored within your very own being, in your very own cells. You may gain information by tapping into other realms of existence, those realms that you know exist but not in the earth plane type of existence. You delve into these realms to gain a better understanding of your inventions, so to speak. You have the capacity to tap into multiple dimensions at the exact same moment because there is no such thing as time. Release the notion that you need to know everything. You came here to understand creation so you can move forward into developing new creations.

As you sit and contemplate this information, close your eyes, just close your eyes. Each one of you reading or listening to these words will see something different. That is because each of you came to create something different. This is such a magnificent organization of beings! There is no reason for two of you to have the exact same experiences. There may be some that are similar, but no two can be exactly alike.

These times you call the new millennia are those years when you said it shall be done. This coming together of mass minds from all creations are here now on this beautiful planet you call Earth. The many minds, your heart's part of your total minds, are you, the composite of you. When you address those whom you feel are your brothers and sisters, you are indeed addressing yourself! This one composite mind of All That Is is! Each of you is just a part of the whole. Let us address those many parts of you who you call your individualization's.

Each one of you has your own soul. A soul is defined as the total you. You see it as your being an individual. Again you are that but part of a larger family of souls. And that family of souls is part of a larger family who again is part of even a larger family, and so on. Creator has divided itself and continues to divide itself ad infinitum. Therefore you, being part of Creator, are continually dividing to create more experiences. Some of your creations are "short-lived" using your vernacular. Other creations continue to grow. All creation is in the creative mind. It is an illusion, yet very real because it becomes or is a part of you.

Each one of you resides in many realms all at the same time because time is vertical. So you create in all realms simultaneously and each realm affects the other. As you grow in your knowledge in one realm, then all realms are benefit of that growth. We call it growth for that is an easy term for you to understand. In actuality, it just is experiences, a part of creator (you) understanding creation as yourself! This, my friend, is the wealth of creation.

An opportunity exists that has never existed before (yes, we are speaking linear now). This is the time where energies of the moon have created a posturing of souls equivalent to the time/space portal of soul travel while inside the human body[2]. This soul travel that you will have the ability to take is your growth into the knowledge of light within light, your ability to activate your merkaba or vehicle of light. This is available to you now, but it will take much growth in your vibratory frequency before this can be totally activated. However, many of you will be able to experience this soul travel while inside your body during this present lifetime.

Furthermore, you will experience a heightening of sensory perception that if activated while in a lower vibratory state would blow your head off. Since none of you really want to do that, then you will receive downloads of higher energy that you will take into your bodies. Work your bodies into fine-tuned health with the release of toxins and bacteria that weigh your bodies down. This is an age where you will want to respect your own bodies and that means honoring all parts of your body and your self! Live with honor for you and all others. Each has her or his own way to become one with all. Each

of you concentrate on your very own selves. This is the way to get through this incredible time to be what Creator meant for itself.

In what you term the near future is the time of total remembrance of you and of God Creator. You shall meet those other parts of yourself. Some of those parts will be by perception only. Other parts will be like meeting another human being, yet you are meeting yourself. That is such a difficult concept for one to take hold of, but after you have done this a couple of times, you will get to understanding the multiple you's.

In this grand world of illusion, you have surpassed the dark days of forgetfulness. Rejoice in the knowing that the road ahead will absolutely astonish your present knowledge of how the universes work. What a wonderful world this will Be!

In Loving Grace, we are the Travelers who are assisting mankind with his remembering.

---

1 See the book *You Are Becoming a Galactic Human* by Virginia Essene and Sheldon Nidle.
2 See Book 52, "The Focus of the Moon," (within this book) for further explanation of the energies of the moon.

June 1, 2007

The Force Field

The force field we are referring to for this book is the force field of each of you divine beings. Everyone has his or her own force field that surrounds his or her physical body. No one is exempt of this field as it is a part of you. It is much more than your merkaba, even though the merkaba is part of that field. This book further explains this field.

In ancient times, or what humans today refer to ancient times, it was known that the body is part of something much grander than what most beings could detect with their physical human eye. So the scientists of that day started a study on this field. It became known as "The Lazarus Papers". The scientists of that day surrendered themselves into the nome position, a position that required them to exit their physical bodies and travel and work in their light bodies. This enabled these scientists to see with their inner eye much like they saw with their outer eye. They also stayed attached to their physical bodies with the use of silver cords. The silver cord is the mechanism that attaches the spirit to the live body. It is an energy attachment that cannot be broken with the life force still viable inside the body. Please note that this silver cord stays attached to the human body for up to three days after the apparent death of the body.

The cyclical body, that of this earth plane, has been an experiment made in heaven. The term "made in heaven" denotes that it was decreed by the beings called the Nefilim, that the higher beings come together in form to promote their own status of creating in the physical the mind control of god infinite. They put themselves in the position to resurrect themselves for their own benefit as well as the beings called the renegades. The renegades are those who decided that their manifestations were incomplete and wanted to work with the Nefilim to play with their own minds of self-service. Thus were the beginnings of the magnificent minds made manifest in the human forms of thousands and thousands of years ago on this earthen plane. The brothers and sisters of the star systems, specifically the Antarees system, made themselves available to this project.

The Lazarus Project began with the condensed energy of the Nefilim form. They created a body within a body within a body. Thus the human form is the inner most body surrounded by the electromagnetic frequencies that closely match that of the earth, and the outer body of the Christed state, the "force field" that can extend wherever the creative mind of the individual projects it to go. This Christed state of being simply is the heightened manifestation of the god force in material form even though it is energy (energy as form). The bubble of biology of the human is, therefore, inside a mecca of divine magnetism inside a sphere of open manifestation to create and move within the extended universe. All bubbles and spheres touch one another and some overlap each other. You are, in totality, One. This project grew into huge proportions and now extends out into new creation that you see as new star systems. This project is ongoing with extensions of this universe as well as new universes within the Great I AM universe.

Time became part of this project, a coherent way to choose one's manifestations. Intermediaries became involved to lend their energies of infinite power, force fields much greater than the original beings involved on the project. This led into another wave of creations. It is like looking into a great sphere of malleable energies moving and undulating at various speeds. This containment of this life force has been changing. It is moving out into new vernaculars into new rhythms. Thus this containment is no more. This is such a monumental explosion of creation, a change for all of creation. The fields are forever expanding, some imploding onto themselves, yet expanding nonetheless. What you are witnessing is the grand explosion of you! Each of you are a part of this new creation and are a partnership in its growth. This time of awakening is for you to realize the enormity of this very project. Your fields touch all other fields. Because of this, you each travel in this body. Your veils are being torn apart so you will consciously understand what you are doing.

When you have achieved the conscious ability to move outside of your physical body, will you know what is before you. You will know the force that you know as God, and you will know that you are part of that very force. If you look at your existent bodies, you will see with your eyes the fields that surround you and all of earth's creations. Now you will understand that these bodies are the mind, the elixir, also known as light, of the God mind, the infinite mind. Yes, your scientists are working to understand this process. Once they see how sound and light, all of the qualities therein, are everything, they will begin to see the relationship of all living things. The sound of OM is the strongest sound of manifestation there is in your world. As you vocalize it in the seven keys, you will note a change in you and about you. Work with this using your waters, metals, and minerals, and you will know the beginnings of this project known as "The Lazarus Effect." Please note that the key of "E" will vibrate the body and enhance the force fields. As you do this, (when using water) watch the undulations of the water ripple outwardly then change course. It will appear that the ripples are moving inward to the center point. The body's center point is the heart, therefore, you will feel a distinct vibration in the heart center. So do not be alarmed of this feeling. Just know that all movement goes into the heart area then out as if moving through a vortex to the "other side." That other side is just another dimension where you will be able to detect other lives and civilizations.

There is a project called the "The Lazarus Project" that is a study on your earth plane today (June 2007). This study involves black holes, the forces of these black holes and how energy is effected. This information being studied by your scientists is actually the study of what we are referring to in this paper. This Lazarus Project has been ongoing for thousands and thousands of your earth years. Scientists reading this – use the seven sacred sounds that you know as the seven musical keys. Now use semi-tones and note the differences in the materials you are experimenting with. Using the key of E, add the harmonic of the heart and note the feeling that you have inside. Hold that resonance and breathe out extending the feeling into your merkaba or close energy field. Now note the vibration you feel in your entire body. With your focussed intent, you can move this energy merkaba and you will feel your body move within this field. You are now in the interdimensional space of cross times or the ability to move into other dimensions with just your intent.

What happens within your bodies happens on a much grander scale (the microcosm and the macrocosm). Therefore you witness black holes within the universe that you can see. These black holes continue everywhere and you will be privy to more of these as the human and other beings of "space" use this technology in creating new creations. Be assured that even though you relate to what is happening here on this planet earth and the other planets in this solar system as well, other solar systems are going through a very similar process of finding that they, too, are part of a much larger process of evolution than they see on their own planets. This process of evolution is forever ongoing but there is a speed-up of technology that is being experienced. As we said earlier in this book, there is newness or a new sense of being that we are all witnessing. What happens next is yet to be decided, but the process has been decided. This process is The Lazarus Project, civilizations going to a whole new level of understanding and a way of being. Enjoy the ride as each of you move through your own "black holes."

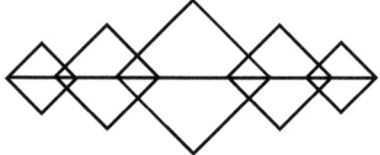

Q – Please explain, in the second paragraph, why it is written "the higher beings come together in form to promote their own status of creating in the physical the mind control of god infinite." Mind control?

A – In essence, it is not control as such by any one being, it is within the whole you create. Mind control used here means beings have the capacity to turn their creations into one of self-service, yet maintain their known connection(s) within the All.

June 29, 2007

The Means of Cooperation

This book explores what it means to cooperate. Do not turn your eye out as we will explain just what this term means. Peace on earth will come when all people will cooperate with one another. This does not mean that one culture is to be subservient to another, but to respect one another's culture. Each of you has so much to learn, and one way to learn is to talk with one another, share. People of this earth, share your thoughts so that you will understand one another. Do not be afraid to share. You will find much peace inside once you understand all cultures.

Understand your abilities, then use them. Your human form is so grand, yet man uses such a miniscule part of their intellectual capabilities. Couple the intellect with the emotional body of yourself, and great thoughts will come to you.

Remember yourself when you were just a youngster learning how to move around, turning, crawling, then standing, all the while quite proud of yourself. You then took the leap and moved using your legs, one foot in front of another. As you continued to explore your surroundings, you found your ability to make objects move as you touched them. You learned the textures, the colors, and the shapes in your new world. You were quite fascinated with this whole new life. Yet part of you still remembered other lives as those images came forward in your mind. Part of you continued in the "old" life until you closed the door on those lives so you could more fully open the world that you just reincarnated into.

All of you living on this earth at this time have lived at least one other life on this earth plane. You are here to experience this shift in your planetary alignment. You volunteered to be a part of what is happening at this time.

Therefore many of you are to purge the old thoughts and life patterns you had become accustomed to in past lives. Each of you are being given the opportunity to move into a new plane of existence. In so doing, it is like going back to being an infant, then a toddler, learning your ways in this new world. It is up to each and every one of you to surrender yourselves from the old patterns into the new. Your old thoughts are to replaced with new ambitions. Your time allowance is getting shorter and shorter. Your earth, lovely Lady Gaia, has made her decision. You can move forward with her or remain behind. It is your choice. If you choose not to go into the higher planes of existence and merge with the other parts of yourself, then you can so choose to do this. You, the soul you, has other avenues to move into for other creations to manifest and explore. However, most of you (all of you who are reading these words) have chosen to move into the emergence of the new kingdom on this earth plane.

Periods of self deprecation, of low self worth are some of the challenges you may endure during this process. The old thought patterns will soon diminish into what can I create Now? A new and exciting time is now and ahead of you.

In the first book "Mystery of the Universes", many of the writings say that you are co-creators with All That Is. You are to go out and create in new worlds. That is correct. Some of your worlds will be right here on this earth. Others of you will decide to incarnate on other planets where you will co-create in whole new life patterns.

Can you now understand what it means to cooperate with yourself as well as with others on this earth plane at this time? You are all going through this process, each processing in a different manner. This is so exciting how this is all playing out. Allow yourself to fantasize, dream, as if you are the fairy tale. Allow others to do just the same. Share your stories if you wish. Do not intrude on another's story unless you are given permission. This is what it means to cooperate. Enjoy this most wondrous world. Know that most of you will move out of the old paradigm of being subservient to those you feel have power over you.

August 5, 2008

Seek and Ye Shall Find

As you travel in your circles you will find that what you seek is always with you and in front of you. Therefore to seek is a misnomer. Perhaps it would be better to say "look" within and the kingdom is yours. Humanity, what is it that you are looking for? Is it heaven, that mystical place where the streets are paved in gold, people are smiling as they skip down this road, or is it nirvana, a state of being that says life is joy? The human when left alone, seeks a better life because they do not realize that they are creators creating their own lives. So really, what is it that you are looking for?

You continue reading, looking for that "thing" that will assist you to be a "better" person. Just what do you mean by the word "better?" What do you want to be better at, better with, better as? Do you understand how confusing you have made your lives not understanding how you create? Just what is better? More money, more food, larger house, loving family, great job, fun vacations? Is that what you mean by better? Please understand the dichotomy that you are producing with these erroneous thought forms. There is no such thing in reality, the real you, that is better. You cannot get any better because you are perfect, always have been perfect, and will continue to be perfect. Many of you say, I am not perfect. Yes you are! Everyone has their own version as to what perfect is to them, or do they?

You would not be where and who you are today if you weren't perfect. All is in perfect order. Oh your earth, that wonderful creature that you live on, is changing because it is her time or moment that she is ready to experience more than she has experienced thus far in her physical life. Yes, many of you humans do not understand what a wonderful being she is as you remove her gases, oils, and rocks from her being. You stick needles into her skin, throw refuge into her seas, and then do not thank her for what she has given you. You may be thinking, this is not being a perfect being, us humans. Yes you are. Are you learning that you are all in this together, each one of you humans, each animal, each plant, each rock and crystal, the soul of this earth? Understand the situation here. Each of you is growing in your beingness, understanding what is means to be a creator. I have heard it said that God is crying because of human's wickedness. There is no such thing! No thing is wicked. You may think that you or another may act wicked, but that path is but a short step into an arena a few decide to tread. You can step out of that arena any moment you decide to create out of love. You know, to create from love is God creating, just God creating.

What humans have devised for themselves! When you see your picture from a perspective not from your human eyes, you see what appears as a comic book. It is not real! So what is really real? Is it you and me and we? Yes. Is it they, them, and the other? Yes. Is it all of us in this together? Yes!

Dear beautiful humans, you have made yourselves quite unique in this cosmic world of form. Each of you live other lives in many other forms. Some of you have memory or knowledge of your other lives. Some of you do not. In Reality, it does not matter. What does matter is that you all are dearly loved, made in love by the most magnificent, the all of you combined. So look within your beautiful self and you will understand what you will find.

So be it, you have made it so.

August 7, 2007

The Turn of the Axis

Through the turning of the Earth's axis do humans receive their bounty. When the sun rises and falls, the earth structure takes on a metabolic change. Understand the co-genetics that transforms each and everything that resides on the earthen plane.

Understand that there are twenty ways to comprehend what this universe is, was, and shall be. To put this into simpler terms, we are the generation of beings that will transpose the internal and external structure of this earth and humanity. By this we mean we have the capability to move this system into a more realized system of co-genetic powers for the reinforcement of the biological circuits that run through this system of the cosmos.

Upon the return of the star ship known as The Wandering One, this earth will wobble and shake until it reaches the frequency of the new galaxy. This increase in frequency shall enhance the genetic emphasis on the biological form that includes all matter, human and mineral, on this magnificent planet. The return to the basic building blocks, the human genome will release all diodes that make it possible for disease and sickness to prevail in the animal kingdoms. These diodes have short-circuited the energetic powers of the god within all. This return to the consciousness of the cerebium will enhance and articulate the new way of being in this physical world.

The time will soon come when the earth will do its turning and reforming and swaying. Do not be afraid or you will falter. Be in tune with this earth's energies and you will not feel the oscillations quite as readily as someone who is out-of-tune with this grand planet. One secret to this turning is to co-exist within your many selves as a more conscious being. This gives you the opportunity to leave this existing body at will so your physical body can integrate the ascending energies of the godhead of this creation. Forces that are known to the controls of this galaxy shall make themselves known and they shall descend upon this planet to teach those that remain on the planet the modes to transform their thoughts and co-creative abilities. As such, mankind will witness a tremendous transformation of this species. The soul, or divine, will resonate with the many tunes or higher frequencies of the new system. Peace within the earth and within the human body will be the norm.

Such a transformation in a relatively short period of time, or turning of the earth's axis, is in itself a most wondrous feat. Man of earth, you are definitely not alone. Your space brethren are here and will remain here with you through these processes of transformation. Some of your brethren will remain on this planet with you. Even others from far away galaxies will join in. Know that all is well and all continues within the divine plan of manifestation. So it is.

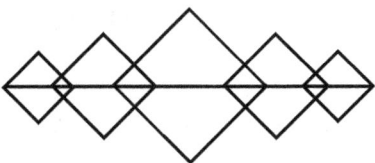

Q – In the first sentence, what is meant that there are twenty ways to comprehend what this Universe is, was, and shall be?
A – The twenty ways includes your multi-dimensionality. Since this life on your earth at this time is very critical for the whole of you and creation, then the twenty ways includes the whole

of you. To break this down further, at this time, would not make sense to you.

Q – In the first paragraph of this writing, it is stated that "we are the generation of beings that will transpose the internal and external structure of this earth and humanity". Who is "we"?
A – We are those beings, some in human form now living on this earth, and those of us who live on surrounding ships or bases as we call them.

Q – Are you known by any name that we can recognize?
A – We are known as The Shining Ones.

Q – Are you The Shining Ones also known as the Elohim?
A – We are.

Q – Please explain the consciousness of the cerebium.
A – The cerebium is that part of the human brain that has lain dormant from its greatest capacity of visualization or manifestation of creation.

Q – In the writing, Book 55, "A Grass Roots Approach," calls the cerebium a brain with one hemisphere.
A – Indeed, the brain will become one hemisphere with so many more capabilities than you presently have.

Q - Light is the arrangement of diodes (see Mystery of the Universes, Book 5 "Book of the Ages II). In this writing, it is written that the basic building blocks, the human genome, will release all diodes that (now) make it possible for disease and sickness. Please further explain.
A – Your bodies, most of you on your planet, are not firing on all circuits and that is when disease and sickness comes in. Part of your energy systems miss-fire, so to speak, or not fire

at all due to blockages from your emotional bodies and also those who have lost parts of their physical bodies. The body was designed to work as a whole, and when the whole does not work all together or in tandem, then you have miss-fires. That is what is meant by the arrangement of diodes that are not working properly.

Q - The Wandering One (or The Wanderer) is returning? Discussed in Mystery of the Universes, Book 50, "Book of the Nightingale," the Wandering One is also known as the star ship "The Lleken" who brought to this planet the knowledge that earth was to be an interface of the divine with the lower thought forms of the Legion. First of all, all is divine. The daughters of The Lleken mated with the gods of Turan, also known as the Anunnaki or Legion. The lower thought forms refers to the Legion's advanced technology that was not in divine will of Creator Source (thoughts originating through the heart). The Lleken came to this planet because they wanted to mate in order to change the form, which was mostly human, to include a more developed sensory mechanism within the physical body. Any comments on this?

A – Yes, all is divine or part of Creator Source as it can be no other way. The return of The Wandering One is definitely a good possibility but, at this writing, has not been determined because of the advancement humanity has mastered in their frequencies. There remains a close communication and relationship with the Legion, or Anunnaki (The Wandering One), but it has yet to be decided how this all is going to play out since this plan is taking the human form into the higher frequencies, a new way to be in the body. Another way to state this is that the human is taking their own power unto themselves. With the veils drawn, humanity has lived much like slaves not realizing their true potential.

January 6, 2008

The Sands of Time

This book refers to the coming and going of the many cycles you and your dear Earth are passing through. Time as you have learned is not linear but an ongoing progression of life.

In recent ages man decided to bring himself into the new realm of everlasting wisdom. He brought in new frontiers, knowledge of his keeper, knowledge of his being in form to be of servitude to the Father, the Source of All Being. He made a declaration that was to be the beginning of a new way of being, a new way of experiencing, a new way to going within. He saw himself as a conduit, like the light of the newly developed light bulb. In the mysteries that have gone on and not understood throughout the middle ages, man became confined to what he termed the religion of the ages. Religion brought humanity to an age of many misunderstandings, each religion having its own identification. Now those misunderstandings are coming to the point of realization that all is an aggregate of the total mass of the time. An easier way to understand this phenomenon is through the telling of a story. This story is about a boy and his dog.

****

It was in the evening of Aaron's seventh year that he decided it was time for him to explore the woods out back of their cabin. He found that he was big and old enough to explore on his own without the company of his mother and uncle. However, Aaron did take along his companion, Artis, his loving Rottweiler. Aaron first decided to go along the winding path that led to the neighbor's barn. Along the way, Aaron picked up the small pebbles in his path. He put these small pebbles into his pocket to look at after he and Artis returned home. Upon arriving at his neighbor's barn, Aaron spotted the neighbor's cow grazing in the grasses alongside the fence. This cow was alone, the other cows far away in the pastures. Aaron thought to himself, *Why is the cow standing here all alone with no other cows to talk to.* So Aaron and Artis went through the gate in the fence to try to steer the cow to join his fellow cows. But the cow would not move. Aaron tried talking to the cow, but the cow paid no attention. Artis even barked at the cow, but the cow paid no heed.

So Aaron decided to leave the cow be as he as a small boy even with his large dog could not persuade the cow to move. So along the path Aaron skipped keeping pace with his companion, Artis. Soon they approached the wide rushing river, flowing briskly down stream into the small lake. Aaron decided to pull out the small pebbles he'd stored in his pocket. One by one he looked at the beautiful stones, each stone a different shape and most of them even a different color. He thought, *Why are these stones so different from one another?* Some of the pebbles he decided to skip into the waters of the river. The prettier stones, he decided to keep and put them back into his pocket. As the boy gazed into the waters, he could see his reflection. Artis was lapping at the cool clean water quenching his thirst. Aaron could see his dog's tongue as it touched the water. Aaron then thought, *Why is this water necessary for our bodies? What is in this water that quenches our thirst?*

As Aaron thought about the nutrition of water, Artis decided to go further into the water snapping at the small fish that swim in the shallow areas. Aaron then thought, *Why do we need food such as fish to nourish our bodies. What is the reason for all of this?* As Aaron contemplated life, he fell into a deep sleep. Artis came out of the water and lay down beside his friend.

In Aaron's deep sleep, he awoke in his dream. The world he saw in his dream was much different from the world in his waking state. Sure he saw people much like himself and his family. He also saw many animals including dogs and cats. But the animals acted differently in this dream state. They were communicating with the people and the people could understand them! Aaron thought, *This is quite odd. How can animals understand people and people understand animals?*

And at times there was no spoken language, just thoughts transferring between them. *Wow,* thought Aaron as he intently watched this new world. *How can this be?* While still in his dream, Aaron decided to explore this new world. He noticed the lavish parks brimming with flowers. He could see the birds gently moving through the air singing sweet melodies. This looked like such a wonderful world, so loving, so beautiful, that Aaron did not want to leave. But Aaron felt a wet tongue licking his face, and returned to the old world.

Aaron remembered every part of the dream. He wondered how he could go back to that new world. Every day he and Artis would go along the same path, stop and talk to the cows, then sit at the water's edge ready to again go into the new world. One day, Aaron again fell into a deep relaxing sleep, and lo and behold, he was back into the new world. He looked around and could smell the bountiful flowers that were under his feet. Along came a large cow much like the cow that stood along the fence all alone that first day he and Artis went for their first journey by themselves. The cow stopped and asked Aaron for directions. Aaron thought that was funny that a cow would ask for directions. But knowing that this new world was so different than his awake world, Aaron responded to the cow, "Where do you want to go and what do you want to see?" The cow said, "I just want to visit with my family down by the lake." So Aaron told the cow to follow her own sense of smell to find her family. The cow said, "Oh, must I use my own senses in this world, too?" The boy responded with "Yes, you have the same senses in this world as you do in the other world of form." So the cow turned and went the way of her senses, mainly that of her olfactory organs.

The boy and his dog thought it was funny that the cow didn't know that she could use her sense of smell in the other world. At that moment, both Aaron and Artis opened up their full senses of smell. In fact, their sense of smell was even stronger than that same sense in the awake world. As they pondered this, they then sensed the true beauty of their surroundings. They could see the undulations in the petals of the flowers. They could see the life flow through every leaf. They could see the emanations from the many rocks and pebbles that lined their path. *What a wonderful place,* they mused. *Why is this world so much clearer in its presence than our awake world?*

As they pondered this some more, they heard a loud booming voice. They turned and saw a most wonderful creature staring at them with a most awe stricken look on its face. However, both Aaron and Artis were not afraid. This creature looked at them with wide eyes knowing that he had come upon new life forms he had not seen before. This creature spoke to both Aaron and Artis, but he spoke with his mind. The creature said: "Who are you and where are you from?"

Both Aaron and Artis visualized their Earth home very similar to where they were standing yet so much different. The creature seemed to understand and said: "Welcome to our kingdom." Aaron said, "Thank you, but where are we?"

The creature responded by saying, "You are in the world form called Fantasia, a most wonderful world of life."

Aaron responded "Yes, this is a most wonderful world. This world is so much alive. The colors are brighter, the air is so clean, and you can see life in everything!" The creature said, "Aye, there is life in everything. It can be no other way. Every stone, every tree, every flower, every animal, and even the bright stars that line our skies are very much alive. Each of us in this world, Fantasia, know that we are here to experience life in reverence to all life, whatever form that may be. This makes this world so happy because we all share with so much love. That is what makes this place so alive because it is so alive. Is this different than your world you call Earth?"

Both Aaron and Artis then realized that their Earth was not so much different, but they had not seen that all on Earth was alive, yet they knew it could be no other way, just as the wonderful creature had said about his world. Aaron then mused, *Why are we on earth not able to sense all life on earth as in Fantasia?*

At that moment Aaron awoke and he and Artis just stared at one another, knowing they both were involved in the same dream. At that moment, the world in the eyes of Aaron and Artis changed forever, for they knew that they were a part of a most wonderful existence.

****

Through the sands of time shall each and every life form know itself as part of a most magnificent world, one in which it has created in the total matrix of all there is. Is life on earth any different than life on Fantasia? Awaken, dear ones, to the real world. Look with new eyes, perhaps just as Aaron and Artis did in the above story. Soon all your visions and your other senses will open to your new world.

November 24, 2007

Book of Generations

It was a millennium ago the star makers and shape shifters turned their attention to the details of this planetary system that includes your planet Earth. By the term star makers, we conclude that these beings forecasted their awareness' to the entities of planetary influences. Their role was the selection of frequencies needed to obtain residence on this planet. In order for one to maintain a residence, one had to reconfigure their atomic body to that of the frequency of the planet so that they could maintain a symbiotic relationship. Thus life on this planet became a part of the curriculum of life inside a biological humanistic body.

Future probabilities are those sequences in a life stream that interpret the frequencies in which a part of their being inhabit. All of creation is One or a total of its parts. So each aspect of a being is the total of the sum of its parts. Each part is introduced into various frequencies to obtain the challenge and the liberty of being, a state of being in the physical or non-physical. Source is made up of all that is physical and non-physical. It is the All yet it is No-thing until it decides to move within its being. To accomplish this feat, it knows that it exists and spews out itself into its many parts. It declares of itself yet the motion that is exhibited is the movement of its minute particles. What happens is the result of the minute particles combining into an energy of fusion.

Many systems have developed through this mechanism of movement. The consistency of the movements bring together the parts in an organized way to evoke what is called life. This new life is then divided many times with each part knowing of itself as part of something much larger than itself. Thus you have emotion or energy in motion. Within this energy in motion, the various particles or energy move and split, move and split, and move then split. Thus the many divisions of One. Through the many splits, it is ad infinitum, particles vibrate at a "speed," thus like particles attract those that are in sequence with themselves.

This is the beginning of life. Those particles that flow in sequence are the bodies that make up what is called the universe, or one "verse" or likeness in their motion. (Also known as light and sound.) The intrusion of unlike particles can cause rifts or tears within a universe. The higher or faster movements can zip right through the slower frequencies, but the slower frequencies cannot go through the higher frequencies (it is like hitting a solid wall). Therefore the higher frequencies can change, move, or manipulate the lower frequencies, thus change life in those lower frequencies. Many universes are formed in this manner. All universes are always changing, moving, or splitting as creation unfolds its energy in motion.

In the physical form these energies of emotion or energies in motion make up the always moving and changing living forms. Therefore life only exists in each sequence. There are then generations of movements known in the physical world as one life, one aspect of the total being. Within each one aspect, the viewer (one inhabiting the physical body) sees itself as whole or a single being. When that being is crossed with the higher frequencies, it then is split and sees itself as more than one personality. Therefore you have the sequences of living life that move about to bring the total life form, physical and non-physical, into a body of refined energy and matter. This family you call You is a part of the family of all living life that is termed God.

To put this concept into a more understandable form, consider that you are just a cell within a whole or large being. Without you, the one cell, the whole being cannot exist for loss of any one part is not possible. However, you, the one cell, communicates with the other cells so the total being is One cohesive Being. Suppose that this One Being decided to find out what it is like to enter into another force, another plane just to discover what it would be like in another "space," something new, added excitement. This something "new" is exciting, like exploring yet the space isn't yet created because the One Being is creating it as its thoughts unfold. There is no one telling this One Being how to be! So as One Being communicates within itself, all of its cells are listening. This sets up a whole new patterning within the One Being.

Now to bring this understanding into terms you on the earth plane can understand, this One Being is You, God creating. All of your "cells" or aspects of you are communicating with one another. Some of you feel like your mind and emotions are on overload because of your newfound awareness of You All as One Being. Please keep in mind that it is your total mind that is at the controls.

You are entering into a new day. So be it as you have created it so.

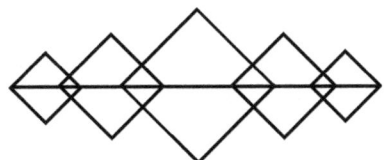

Q – The sentence that says that our "total mind that is at the controls." I understand our thoughts become things, we create our own reality (most used phrase), and this book says much the same thing, however it is explained much more fully. Our total mind is at the controls. Please explain how this relates to us as "separate" (how we see ourselves) humans creating our own reality.

A – To answer your question, you do understand that you are not separate.

Q – Yes, I do understand that being separate is impossible.

A – Therefore your current life stream you see as separate is a part of the total You. Your choices in this life affect the All of You (the many parts of Your Self). Let go and let God is another way of saying that you submit to your Higher Self, the god that you are. You have a "contract" to be in this bodily form. And this contract is one you devised to learn and experience life in this biological bubble. The All of You have a say so in what you want to experience, and you put on the blinders to experience this biological life without realizing you are part of something much grander. Can you now understand how and why your Whole Self is involved? You still have choices to make while you are in biological bubble of physicality. You gave yourself free will. You still are connected to or a part of You. The All of You work (live) in tandem. And your All of You work in tandem with all the other All of You's, the One or Source.

January 25, 2008

The Walk

Through the passing of what you call time, this book describes the return of the You.

Pieces of each one of You are here on this earthen plane manifesting at a rate so expedient that many of us on the other planes of existence have our heads spinning, using your vernacular. You have survived the litmus test making this part of humanity into something so much more than the original design of the species.

This original design was to incorporate the fingers of control, but not in the sense of controlling your every move for that would eliminate why this process was even started. No, we are talking about control in that You are made with your biology connected, or better said, a part of the kingdom of heaven, God Creator in All. You set the stage for this play to continue until you have received all the nuances, all the joy, all the pleasure out of being human. Most of you have come from the many star systems that you see in your skies. You did not originate here on this earth, for that would be an impossibility as each one of you were in existence long before this planet earth came into being. You are asking, what happens now?

Imagine a place so grand, so wonderful, with every one of your senses stretched to encompass your whole world. Each of your senses, the six of them (so far), is so sensitized that you literally feel that you are in another time and space. That is your new paradigm. You will be in another time and place. Your world is changing its face and body to capture a new essence. You are not going back to where you have been, but going boldly into where you haven't been before. Your movies and television shows have captured some of what we are talking about.

Each one of your minds is reconnecting consciously (you have always been connected) to that All of You. Soon you will realize your magnificence! We understand that you have been told this, but do you comprehend what all of this means? You are returning to live in your god essence, each one of you separate yet so much a part of the whole. Your ability to know the whole of All, yet you will still process or create New.

To understand this more fully, you are boldly going where no man has dared to go. They have not dared because they did not know of the possibilities. Your fears of the unknown will soon vanish and not to return as you enter in the fifth paradigm more fully. You will continue on the precipice until you are ready to make the leap. You will not fall but fly within yourself to this new reality. How joyous this is as you interlock your arms and do this swiftly and together. The gate is cleared. You are the only one who can make this decision to fly.

Okay, now what? Yes, we tell you all of this is happening, yet you feel that this process is too incredible. It isn't. You all are incredible. Once you realize that this is so, you will fly. In the mean time, continue on your daily walks of life but with a new sense of what is real. Ask your senses to move up a notch so that they can evolve into this new way of Being. The trumpets have long ago sounded and each of your lips were on the horn. Love one another as each of you continues through this process. See your fellow man no less or no more than you. Soon you will discover a new principle, love only You!

February 20, 2008

An Arm's Length Away

You are just an arm's length away from being the true being that you really are. You are reconnecting your consciousness to the All That Is. As you continue on this reconnection, you will find that your sensory system will feel like it is on overload. It is not. What determines this feeling is your acceptance of the fact that you indeed are the renaissance of humanity, making your way into the great unknown of biological life. To reach into this unknown, you are giving up the old processes that you had developed for yourselves. The old processes include the detainment of all of your faculties, using your biological systems in a more robotic fashion.

This use of your being has propelled you to a new level bringing all of You into alignment. As discussed in earlier books, there are many of you experiencing reality in a multitude of ways. Reality, therefore, is what you make it to be. The understanding of this phenomenon will be clearly seen as you project your new thoughts in the new screen of your new lives. You control the dials, the levers, all what makes up each one of your realities.

As you move to your new positions, you will find that some of your levers will no longer work. Some of your buttons will not work. What reality are you choosing when you try to use those levers and buttons? Perhaps that is the reason for breakdowns. As you play in your old and new worlds, you will find some difficulties in the controlling functions. That is because some of the old controls do not work in the new world and the new controls do not work in the old world. Makes sense? Each of you has been living in two worlds, the you that is the bubble of biology that you know yourself as a human to be. When you stop playing at the controls in both worlds, will the old robotic world disappear and the new world come in with sharper focus.

This new world is your new utopia. It is a most wondrous world, where you humans will play determining what game you want to play next. Your options are endless. Your creations are unlimited. There will be nothing that says that you cannot do this or that because that is a foreign concept in this new world. Soon you will forget the old world as your memories will fade fast. That is okay because if you did not participate in the old world, you would not be in the new world. How great is that?

These times that are now are momentous! They are momentous in that you are surviving both worlds, the all of each one of You. Sure many of you will decide to work on the "other side", that side where you leave your biological human body and float around deciding if you want to participate in the new world or go on to another world, whatever the dimension you wish to play in. Keep in mind that you have a mind and you have a heart-mind. Create wisely from the heart-mind and your mind will be in ecstasy! No sensory overload, none of that. However, you senses will be so heightened that you feel like you want to jump out of your skins. And you know what? You will be able to jump out of your skins, and you will be able to get right back into those very skins. How cool is that?

You and your world are so close to the juncture of you leaving the old world behind and hopping on the new Earth with both feet firmly planted. Your new creations will be beyond your wildest dreams. That is why you want to dream wildly! Your technological advances will be enormous. Your own biological technology will be incredible. Know that this is the way and there is no turning back. Come join You in your New World.

The season of time is ending. Welcome into the new paradigm of new technology. An arm's length away will have new meaning. Contemplate that! We love you.

January 21, 2008

The Currents of Today

What is meant by "today"? Today is yesterday's tomorrow and tomorrow's yesterday. So today is where you are living in this moment, in this form. It is your January 21, 2008, on your Gregorian calendars, but so what? What does that mean? Perhaps your Gregorian calendars are just your measurement of time seeking to understand itself.

In the far out reaches of your Universe are the heavens. You will find heavens after heavens, living beating parts of life, always evolving, always moving. Hear the beat of the hearts of these far out there universes. Their aliveness are no more than your aliveness and also no less. They are all a part of the Grand Creation unfolding in their creations.

Today mankind you are moving quite rapidly through the heavens that you have seen as your tomorrow. When you can envision your current world the same as you envision tomorrow's world, then you will reach the point of creation where time is no more. It is a step into the far reaches of the heavens (the higher frequencies) yet you remain right here on this earth. You have made it. You have transcended. You are NOW in the 5th dimension. Does the world look or feel any differently to you than fifty years ago or even five years ago? Some of you will answer yes, it is much different. Others of you will see no change, except perhaps in your technologies. Then why do some of you notice great changes while others do not notice change at all?

Welcome to the new world. This new world is the world of change, however each of your perceptions is different because each of your creations are different. All of you gods have your own creations and each of you have chosen this earth and "time period" in which to experience your creations. Throughout your lives you may have noticed that you weren't on the same page as many of your fellow man. Wouldn't life be a bit boring if you all are on the same page? "On the same page" is taken from your vernacular in which the word page means the same thought patterns or belief systems. So why are we all here experiencing life on different pages now?

Life, this sacred part of our being, has come to the understanding that this biological life is a precursor to a new way of life, perhaps a whole new page. Wow! Your new pages are blank, ready for you to write the script. Yet you feel parts of you who are in your future, your tomorrows. If your future is not yet written, then how can those of us who reside in the future exist or be? Such a conundrum of thought! In linear time, that is not possible. So Creator does not reside in linear time. Since you each are a part of Creator, then you do not reside in linear time.

This thought brings in a whole new way of thought, does it not? If you aren't linear, and you are changing with tomorrow not yet written, then how do we change our thoughts? You have been doing it one step at a time. There is that "time" word again. You have been changing your thoughts as you combine your thoughts into the hologram of All That Is and you are changing your old hologram. Your currents are changing. You will witness your life in a whole new way!

In order for this change to happen for each of you, is to let go of the old patterns. This change will allow the new patterns to be established within each one of you. When this happens, you will see yourselves in a whole new way. One main constant for each of you is the vibration of love. The old patterns of duality are fading as the old matrix is being transmuted into a higher frequency. The higher currents called love are sweeping through the old matrix washing out any stuck patterns of behavior that is detrimental to your being. Each of you will continue to have your own creations but you will see them in a whole new light! Some of you will wake up in the morning and your world will have changed. For others of you, the process will take longer until you can be in that place of today with no tomorrows or yesterdays. Contemplate this. Allow the divine thought patterns enter into all parts of yourself, then you will witness your new world.

March 9, 2008

An Encounter with Yourself

It is with delight that we bring to you a summary of You. Each of You has brought into this lifetime that you now live an abundance of knowledge from the many realms from which you all have come. Be gentle on yourself as you move this information to the forefront of your being.

It is with much discernment that we bring to you the following information. What we mean by discernment is that most of you reading these words will completely understand what is being shared while a few others will be totally turned off by such information. We bring you this information to open yourselves even wider to the understandings of your divinity.

We start with the clearing of any preconceived ideas you have of yourself and why you feel that you are divine. See a blank screen in front of you. Slowly a picture will form on the screen. Look closely at the screen. Keep in mind that all who are reading this will have different pictures on your screens so there is to be no comparisons. Watch closely as your screen gets wider and wider and wider. Soon the screen has encompassed you, this biological bubble of you. What you see, feel, experience in this screen/bubble is your individual experience. Each of you is in your own bubble with a different screen playing a different tune, a different sequence of events.

As you watch your movie play out, observe yourself in this movie. Feel, see, hear all the goings on, the emotion of your body, the truths that are being played for you to experience. As you continue to observe yourself, notice others within your movie. Note what they are doing, seeing, believing, judging (yes, judging) for their own growths. Can you now understand this great experiment? Can you watch your own movie and note how it is being played out? You are the director. You are the producer. You are the actors/actresses (to be gender kind even though in the non-illusional world there is no gender). As you observe your experiences, observe You, your god-self. What do you see and how does this make you feel?

Mankind of this earthly realm, remove those blinders that have kept you in darkness. Remove those old paradigms that have kept you in limitation. Remove those blinders that have kept you from your Higher Self. Remove those blinders that have kept you from your connection with Source, the Source that is You! Upon this removal of the illusions you have built for yourself, see You as the totality of Source. There is One Source and you are that One Source. You All are that One Source. However, You shall remain as a division of Source to bring to Source the knowledge that All is Divine.

You are entering into a new kingdom (movie) you have built for yourselves. You have given yourselves the knowledge that greatness has nothing to do with your acts but how you have moved, grown, worked with those acts. Now those acts are making themselves a new creation. Creation is renewing itself through you. It is creating and creating and those creations are becoming your wide screens, much like your wide screen televisions yet in a multi-world way.

You will be able to manipulate those screens to enhance the total image of Source. You are in control only through your god-self. Yet you think you control your current material world through this biological body. You do not. Listen to your god-selves and you will begin to see the whole of you. From this viewpoint, you will be able to move your creations into being in whatever realm you want to play and you will be doing this consciously. It will seem like new technology yet this technology has always been a part of you. You are just beginning to tap into this technology.

Recognize You. Recognize yourself as the Supreme Being. Recognize yourself as part of all of creation. As you recognize your god-self, you will be able to tap into many forms of existence, past, present, and future, all dimensions in which you live.

To those of you who are saying that this cannot be, it is alright. Know that all is in divine order and done only through Love.

April 3, 2008

Love in Action

It has been prophesized that man would be the center of attention as he comes into his being and realizes that he carries within him the greatness of creatorship. He has the ability to proclaim his fire, his determination into life so grand that it will take eons of time for him to fully understand those capabilities.

Understand the peculiarities that are in place for Creator to understand Itself in the image of man. It has determined that the Will set within the soul constructs is so powerful that the soul itself explodes into its many factions. It is and ever shall be, in its infinite wisdom of maintaining a circuitry of multiple lives, one stacked upon another yet seemingly separate. This placement of multiple soul lives is the genesis of Creation. Creation in and of Itself is an expression of the Force of All That Is.

What is happening on the plane of Earth, 3rd density, is the recall of mastership. In order for this recall to manifest itself is for the 3rd density to fade and let the 4th and 5th densities appear. This shedding of the skin, so to speak, is the release of particles held within the confines of duality, within the spectrum parlayed upon the planet Earth. This shedding shall come about with the release by Earth Mother, our Lady Gaia, in her ascension into the new Earth, her partner that is also she. The metamorphosis of the planet shall take the human and her inhabitants on a journey into the upper realms of manifestation. In order to do so, she must rid herself of the fine densities that have held her captive to the lower realms of creatorship. As she sheds her coat of duality, she releases into the more refined dimensions her ability to bind her love with other great beings that are celestial stars and planets. Her ability to become as a star is her next step in her own understanding of herself.

Upon her surface shall she inherit the forces that Creator Love has to offer or, to understand it, to just BE. She breathes a lightness and that light manifests into the dream reality of pontification. She becomes the dreamer and the dreamie. She becomes the factor for creation to hold the magnificent energies of multiple creations – not only humanity, but ultra-humanity. The symbology becomes the reality with the movement of matter, those finite particles that are the constructs of biology. Upon the surface of the new reality will the particles coagulate into new ideas, into new technologies that heretofore have not been part of this Earth.

To explain ultra-humanity is like trying to explain what is the position of the sun, the stars, the position of the cosmos. It is here, still here, within the constructs of time and space, yet is elusive in the explanation of what is. Ultra-humanity is man, still in his biological form, yet not the form of yesteryear. This new form has the ability to transform its thoughts into new forms of manifestation, all together with the manifestations of its fellow man coupled with "man" not of the earth (at this moment).

The ultra-human will soon realize its potential and will be able to cross the time lines/matrixes, thus travel through "space" as "space" will be viewed in a whole other dimension/dimensions.

Humanity, understand that this new day is upon you. It is entirely up to you to embrace the love that you are, made possible through the totality of Love, the consciousness of this universe as well as the consciousness of all other universes tied together as the One. Shed your density as that of the snake. See your new skins as they glow emanating you the master. Know that the new time is here, the here and now. It is up to you to grasp yourselves wholly (holy) and unconditionally. What you dream, you are. You are in charge of you and know that you are a part of the total You. You are love in action.

June 9, 2009

The Mother

The bountiful Earth, the great structure that you stand on, is breaking into the new form of creation. Her skin is shaking and moving, breaking forth the newness of being. She has spoken of the day when all is to be made new, new in the grandness of being. She knows of herself as the one who shall bring her inhabitants with her as she releases the old rags of yesteryear, those energies of lower vibration she will not and cannot take with her into her new state of being. She has declared herself the deliverer of mankind as she takes her stand, the star among the stars she feels a closeness to.

She communicates with many star systems as she bows in reverence to those who have gone before her making the path easier to travel in the grids of creations. She understands her role as the peacemaker. She understands her fortitude in the knowledge as she takes the steps to deliver the people into a new time, a new way of life. She knows what she must do to bring the justice deserved by those who have tarried in her trenches to find out that they were the ones who had built those trenches. These trenches are no more, there is no need for them. The people, humankind, on this Earth shall surrender to the new way of life, the new way of being. They shall only live from their heart of hearts as they move their creations into a lock of love. They shall know of their ancestors, for, indeed, they are their ancestors. Creation shall manifest openly and without denial, for such things will not be part of the new consciousness.

The heart of our dear Mother Earth has opened to receive the blessings of the One. She understands that it is she that shall lead into the new realms. Her heart beats as a beautiful rose opening to let all light shine within her. Mankind shall know of her love, and that, indeed, she is alive and well and knows of herself as that divine spark. Man will coordinate his activities with her heart. There will only be respect, one for the other and the other for the One. She communicates with man and they will be able to hear her and feel her warmth. There will be no questions in this communication, for man will understand.

This dear Mother now takes her place in this cosmos of creation listening to the echoes emanating throughout the webs, or matrices, from which the form is built. It is through the thoughts of the All that the All exists in the many forms. She shall hear only those tones that vibrate their beingness from the realms of the higher heavens. This most powerful being now has made her call to say that it is she that must move on, to that place she knows as star light. She has become this star leading the newborn of auxiliary creations into a new light of love made manifest in the seventh heaven of life.

August 7, 2007

Resurrection of the Mind, Body, and Spirit

Approximately two million years ago on this earthen plane there existed a colony of exploration by highly evolved beings. These beings came here for the purpose of discovery of the balance between the forces of the planetary worlds and the interplanetary world (or the world within this planet). Their mission was to understand the logistics of interplanetary cycles, their effects on this earth, and the effects on other planets, those close by such as within this solar system as well as planets outside of this solar system. Their findings are within this book. The records of this writing can only be accessed through the Akashic Records and the Hall of Records.

The means to accomplish why we came to this earthen planet is through our own interpretation of the fields that meet and cross throughout this creation. There exists a lattice of rays of energy that encircle this blue planet, and these fields touch other fields that are a part of this solar system of magnetic endorphins. This solar system, in turn, is within the parameters of the ones who have planted the seeds of knowledge to take this planet into a regime of photosynthesis of the body's mechanism of divine articulation. The means to accomplish this is through the connective cycles that this planet is to go through to reach its pinnacle of form. This form is to accommodate the body of various species made in the likeness of the various creator gods. Their fusion of the mind shall make this planet unique in that the celebrated activities of the mind made manifest is at the hands of the beloved ones who also call themselves the Magnificents. These beings are part of a much wider organization that includes the recipients of the lost worlds, those worlds who could no longer hold their form, therefore these forms either exploded or imploded.

 The current of these lost worlds still resides in the ethers of this solar system. The bodies of these worlds have been strewn through this system and continue to burn with the entering of their parts into the atmospheres of the more solid planets. The activities which caused these explosions and implosions brought to this system the necessary beings of light to begin a process of reformation. So the human today, this day in the year 2007, is the recipient of the forces who maintain their presence to bring about global change and interstellar change. The many sorrows that resulted from the explosions will return to the unconscious mechanisms of the mind and be transmuted into light energy. The forces of the Magnificents shall make themselves known at this turn of the millennia and they will find themselves remaking this world in its original form. What this means is that this form, this fine Earth many call Gaia, will be remade as it once was two million years ago. The old lands will again resurface, and some of the current lands will again seep under the seas. This planet is to be made new but in the likeness of its original form.

 What shall happen to the inhabitants of this planet is that they too, will go back to their original forms, made in the likeness of their creator gods. They will reconnect their minds with their bodies and be open to all communication from their creator gods. They will be fully conscious beings within the physical form.

Nothing shall come in the way of this great transformation. All residual effects from the one's who brought with them their tyranny, shall vanish. All will be made new. All strife, hunger, poverty, and the like will no longer be tolerated on this planet. The other planets within this solar system will likewise be made new and return to their pristine conditions as they continue on in the life of these worlds. New frontiers of planetary systems are forming and these gods of this planet Earth will be the caretakers of these new systems. You will know who you are and when you will be called to take your new positions. A new day is dawning.

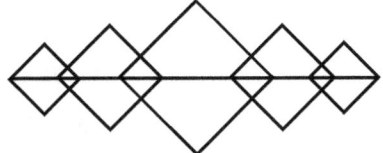

Q – In the preface of this writing, it is stated that this book is to be found in the Akashic Records and The Hall of Records. However, within its text, it is written for today. Please explain.
A – Yes, it is written in the Akashic Records as well as The Hall of Records. However, these records are the past, present, and the future.

Q – What is meant by "solar system of magnetic endorphins" (paragraph one)?
A – Your solar system is part of a much larger system of planets and stars that make up what you call The Milky Way. Within your tiny solar system lie many magnetic fields that criss-cross as a lattice. Therefore, all of your planets are very closely related and each one planet within this solar system greatly affects the other planets. Therefore, "magnetic endorphins" are those webs or lattices of connective magnetic frequencies, the endorphins relating to the infrastructure of this lattice. These lattice infrastructures are made of frequencies that become the

painkillers for your individual planets.

Also, endorphins are a body's own natural painkiller, a hormone secreted by the anterior portion of the pituitary gland (inhibits the perception of painful stimuli). Therefore, in this instance, this writing speaks about your solar system's magnetic endorphins, these endorphins (magnetic waves) obscuring what may seem painful to the whole Self, the 3rd dimensional human. It may seem painful to many when they are not living (perceiving) their divine life, who they truly are. Living on Earth and in other parts of this solar system is very difficult for the soul (whole Self) to take on, yet a process deemed necessary to bring the soul into a better understanding of their totality.

Q – Also in paragraph one, this planet is to be taken into a "regime of photosynthesis of the body's mechanism of divine articulation." Please help us understand what this is saying.
A – The word "photosynthesis" derived from the Greek word meaning "light" and "putting together" is a process that converts carbon dioxide into organic compounds using the energy from sunlight. Regime means mode. Therefore, this is another way of saying that how the human body is to work with light, a "food" to make it work (divine articulation). Very simply said is that this planet will hold those frequencies that will maintain the body in full consciousness of the fifth dimension.

Q – In Book 13, "The Walk," it says humanity is so much more than the original design of the species. The writing above says "the inhabitants of this planet…will go back to their original forms." Is there a discrepancy here?
A – Forms and designs are two different things. The original design was made then genetically altered many times, thus the original "forms" (there were many) were changed. Since the collective human you know today is made up of a combination of many star systems, each one of humanity will start taking

on a new appearance going back to their original forms (when they came to Earth) made in the likeness of their creator gods. However, as a collective, humanity has come a long way in their transitioning.

December 7, 2009

The Unicorn

This figure you know as the unicorn is a fabled creature in many of your stories you call fairy tales. Tales they are, but their existence is far beyond any fictional book. It is time to understand some of these fabled tales and let you know that they are a part of this earth and again will come into existence very soon. All creation is through the mind, the creative heart/mind exists as creation projecting. In other words, it is through the humans' projections along with the other aspects of their being, to bring into this Earthly creation, the creature known as the unicorn. The horn over the third eye is like a conduit of sorts, where it can determine its location anywhere on the Earth plane by focussing through the energetics of earth's ley lines. It is like a radar of sorts, feeling the love of the earth and the run of the electromagnetic frequencies through the skin of the planet. These animals will be of great service to mankind as they integrate their own abilities to maneuver over the earth. Your horses have some of these abilities now, but the intensity that the unicorn displays will be of great service in your near future.

This unicorn will be developed through your sciences, genetically combining DNA to again produce such an animal. It has been done before and is being done again. Even though this project is being created through the use of your test tube sciences, it is no accident that this project is being worked on now. You will soon hear bits and pieces of this experiment before the unicorn creature is shown to the world. This experiment will be scoffed and laughed at, but in the end, these animals will bring a new dynamic to the people of this Earth. They will be like teachers when they are released into the wilds. Their movements will be tracked and the observers will notice a pattern in these movements. The animals will trace the earth's ley lines in a pattern. The pattern will be documented and the scientists will notice the synchronicity in this pattern. An interesting aspect of this project is the knowledge that will be gained as this pattern is projected over the world map, detailing all the key points of transfiguration from the ancient maps to the current map.

What man will realize is the points are major vortices connecting our earth to the planets within our solar system as well as connecting to the other planetary systems involved with humanity. These points are much like star gates, higher intensity frequencies that will enable the lift-off of ships that will become prominent in the future as earth man becomes accustomed to the off-world beings that will make themselves known and share in their technologies. The location of these vortices has not changed since the creation of Earth into its solid form. The earth has changed many times since its creation and will continue to change in its magnetic structure, giving movement to its land and waters. Your compasses will continue to change as true north changes constantly. Be not alarmed as this process has continued throughout the life of this planet, an incarnation of Lady Gaia.

When viewing the pattern of these vortices, you will notice a "belt" around earth's girth. Each of these points is a conduit of the higher frequencies and they interconnect within the skin of the earth causing a powerful light to explode within the inner earth. This enables Lady Gaia to breathe as she propels herself in this dimensional shift to new energies and to her new position within this solar system and the cosmos.

This project has started but will not be introduced to the world until humanity is ready to understand what is happening in this great shift. We are pleased to present this information to you so that you know that this project is not a hoax and shall be completed at its designated moment.

April 3, 2008

Creation within Creation within Creation within Creation

There comes a time when all is made new. All is made new in the sense that the "new" all is not the same as the "old" all. This is the process of ascension that you and your planet are going through at his time.

Man, in his endeavor to understand the newness of being, stands in the room that he perceives himself to be. To be is that essence he sees himself, his beingness. Yet his beingness is so much grander than his ability to grasp within his mind and heart. However, when using the heart as the means to understand, man will move closer to understanding his total essence, and that essence is part of multiple dimensions. The founding fathers (sources) of humanity are within the make-up of humanity. They are in the genes, the chromosomes that make up the physical being, and in the energy fields of each being. They are in the skeletal body that make up the matrices of the various dimensional planes. They are in the workings of the movement of all living things. And everything everywhere is living.

Man, listen to that inner voice that calls to you. Listen to what that voice has to say. You, indeed, will remember and understand these other lives, all of them, all phases, all types. Types? Once you realize that you are not only in the human body, you are also in a multitude of bodies. Some of these bodies are more dense than others, but they all make up the total you. To describe some of these bodies, we shall first let you discover that you also exist everywhere, everywhere within the Total Being you call Source. Source is All so that makes you a part of the All. The All is always expanding yet remains in the context of Its own Self. Source breathes and extends within like an expanding balloon, but space doesn't exist beyond the boundaries of the balloon. To understand this concept is to understand the unlimited boundaries because the balloon never quits expanding. The foreverness is this All.

You on the other hand have come into this region of the matrix of space and time to bring about a balance to the lower worlds of form. Your connectedness to the All and within the All is involved. This process of duality has brought to the forefront of this living life in the lower dimensions a prospective of the grandness of Being. Life on this Earth has become such a magnet of insecurity and obscurity, yet with the help of many of you humans, you have survived the human holocaust, ready to understand other points of life and light. You have seen the rise and fall of many empires, and you know that your existence involves all kinds of species on this earth and throughout all of the cosmos. Now you are ready to turn your attention (consciousness) inward, into that new state of being. The rapture is approaching where all of mankind will find himself in new territory. You still will have choices how you want to live, but you will relate to your fellow man in a whole new way. In fact, all life including the life of this earth, your dear Lady Gaia, is making this shift. Relationships will take on a new meaning in that you will relate to one another and to yourselves in a whole new way.

Beyond the new earthly experience, you will begin to relate to the other aspects of Creator, the consciousness you know as you. You will begin to understand the relationships of the planetary bodies as they move to their rightful places. Your feelings or emotional bodies will transition into nirvana only caring about yourself and your connectedness to your fellow man. In so doing, you will realize that you are your fellow man, and the planets, the animals, the stars, and all the universes. Therefore you will care about the All.

Listen, humans, your time is now that this world is changing and taking shape into the new paradigm of life. You will recognize your fellow beings that you have known throughout the ages, in what is termed no time. Indeed you will feel that you never left, and you have not left, outside the parameters of your human consciousness. You will bring into your human mind these remembrances. It shall be as a homecoming of sorts once your realize the veil has been pulled. You will see the layers upon layers of your very own self, your very own soul that is your god. You will perceive all of you gods, each playing their own instruments. These instruments make up such a beauteous chorus. You will also notice your abilities to create more freely and openly with your thoughts manifesting right before your eyes, in the moment. There will be no lag time as you now experience on your existing earth plane.

Creation is never ending. It is and always shall be. In these turns of events in this sector of the galaxy known as The Milky Way, are changes being made to bring forth the understandings of this Universe as well as others, as the Universes unite. It is the beginning of a new era with a multitude of new experiences (new expressions) within the All of the One. This moment has been foretold and you are now experiencing this moment. Be at peace and know that only love exists in the newness of you.

May 27, 2008

Founding Fathers

In your first book, "Mystery of the Univers-es," you learned (remembered) that humanity is a composite of many extraterrestrial beings who became a part of your genetic makeup. Thesebeings are very much a part of you, not only a part of your DNA, but also a part of You, an aspect of the total You. Many people are starting to see parts of themselves as other than human. Your Founding Fathers (sources) are those other aspects of each one of you, seemingly separate, but an intricate part of the whole. You now have arrived at that place where the experiences in your other lives have an effect on your current earthly human life, and vice versus.

It has been said that the times you call the New Age would be such a transitional argumentable time as the humans who live on the earth plane start to remember the other parts of themselves. At first they will not believe that what they are seeing and feeling are only themselves as they begin to see these other aspects of their total beingness. Confusion will be a great part of this process. Many people will say that cannot be. They will say: "We are totally separate serving our God. We are here on the earth to learn goodness so we can get into heaven for eternity." And we say to you, explain eternity. Just what does this mean?

Eternity is. It is the whole and absolute. It is everything that was, is, and shall be. It is the beginning and the end. Humanity is the beginning and the end. Humanity is in service to its gods, and there are many gods, each god a shining part of Oneness.

As the human develops into a more realized being, that is knowing the other parts of itself, it soon acknowledges the absolute that it is. The human begins to see more fully the connectedness of everything everywhere. The scientists are seeing this in their experiments. Everything everywhere is connected. Soon will this be an accepted phenomena.

So what happens when you connect to the other parts of yourself? You can see from their (Your) eyes, and hear from their (Your) ears. It is much like watching a movie, but you are the star in every movie. Oh you will see others in your movies, and some of the other ones you communicate with you know in your present reality (or the world that you perceive as your existing reality). Many of you are now experiencing this phenomenon. These lives are all of your creations. Do you like the movies that you have produced? Can you pick out anything in each of your movies that really stands out for you? Each life that you live has a message or many messages. You will realize that you have lived the gamut of experiences, ones that you may now perceive as both good and bad. They are neither. They just are experiences.

Many of you are having experiences that make you feel home sick. All of you came from somewhere else other than Earth. In fact, you all have parts of you that come from hundreds of planetary systems, yet one system may seem more like home than others. Some of the home planets have sent out their delegates to live on this Earth plane, experience the combination of the many nations (planetary systems), then report "home." And most of you are those delegates! Of course your soul families are all a part of this game and what a game this is. This game has amazed us all because you have come through such density, such blind vision, yet have come out the other side and been so much richer for the experiences. We ALL are much richer for your and our experiences.

We are here to tell you that your many parts, those original parts of you, are called your Founding Fathers. "Fathers" is a name for Source and nothing more. There is no gender here. In fact, you created gender to know what it is like to live in a left-brained state of mind. You forgot you can create. You created the feminine so you could later recall that you are Creators. Can you now imagine what you have created together?

This book is to remind you that you indeed have a home away from this home. Tune in to your star and let the images pour into you so that you can remember. Your family and friends are cheering you on, can you hear their applause? How do you tune in? Just ask and listen, just listen to that still small voice within. You may "hear" a whisper or a thunderous response. Maintain that connection and you shall know to whom to speak. It may be one star, a part of the Pleiades, Sirius, or Andromeda, or wherever, or many. As you speak your truths about who and what you really are, there is no need to hide or is there need to stand on a platform and speak to the masses. Some of you will speak to the masses to help them understand their Source. Others of you will continue living your lives incorporating the knowledge and wisdom of all of the ages. This Earthen world will unfold to become the most magnificent adventure in all of History. History is your story and your many lives.

We leave you with this message:

Believe that you are God, Source within Source. Know that you are the makers of heaven, your lives on earth. As you transcend the density and see through the veil, you will witness your amazing creations in all their splendor, beautiful colors, beautiful sounds all filled with love. You are that and more. And so it is.

June 19, 2008

The Hearts of Morrow

It has been said that through the heart you shall hear God. This next book teaches that concept more fully. Can you hear yourself speak to you?

The change of time is your change of heart. That does not mean that you change your mind as you think of it on the earth plane. However, as you change your heart, you mind changes with it. Your mind has to follow your heart. That is the way this creation was formed. To perceive is to hear. You hear that inner voice as it tells you what you believe. Oh yes, your beliefs are always changing. Therefore your perceptions are also always changing. You are about to realize this phenomena.

Your overall body of light is made up of many points of light, hence perceptions. To perceive is to acknowledge what you feel you are. As you transcend what you feel you are, then you go onto another perception of who you think you are. Let us give you an example of this idea. Imagine yourself on a boat, sailing in the middle of the ocean looking for land. Yet it has been so long that you were on land, that you forget even what land looks like. So you have a perception of what land is. If there are others on the boat with you, their perception of land may greatly differ from yours. You may perceive that there are large trees, the total tree being green. You forgot that trees have bark, brownish gray in color. So you see your tree totally green. Another on your boat may remember a tree with red leaves with three points on each leaf. As they explain to you what their tree looks like, you cannot comprehend red leaves as you have no memory of such as a thing. You say that cannot be because all you "see" is some type of green foliage. Can you even explain what is foliage? However, your friend can "see" foliage, so they can explain just what a leaf looks like. As you listen to them explain foliage, you start to imagine foliage, yet such a thing is difficult for you to imagine because of your own perception seeing only green. Now the boat sees land or discovers an area without water on it. Those on the boat decide what they see is indeed land. As you look at this land, you will first see the green trees because that is what you had imagined. Your friend will search for the red leaves and see them first, because of what he imagined. Only when you allow yourself to see what another has imagined, will you open to another's perception. Can you now understand what a complex yet so simple worlds you have imagined?

As you see another's perception, or the perception of another part of yourself, will you understand creation. Those perceptions are coming into your view as you become a more realized part of self. Those imaginations are your images you are projecting into your worlds, and you are seeing into more than one world. Your projections combine with your brother's (and sister's) projections and you see yourselves living out God's will. And God's will is your will. It is your projections.

So it is in this day that you project to create tomorrow. Life continues forever more. As you imagine through your heart, new creations come into view for you to experience. Your journey continues ad infinitum. Creator gods, you are incredible beings. Enjoy your journeys knowing that in this process, you are creating life in tandem with all parts of yourself within this Great One that stretches into many aspects called Life.

Whatever you create, it is. The part of you that you call human has reached a plateau where you the human can see your creation unfolding. Welcome all parts of yourself and create in tandem. Creation starts in the heart and goes out from there. You are one, the center of your creation. Feel the joy that you are. Indeed, your human perceptions are changing. Be at peace, and be peace. So be it.

May 13, 2008

A Clear Expression of You

This book explains the term "expression" as this term is used throughout many writings. We who are the Zealots of yesterday understood this term and we were chastised for such thoughts and beliefs. However, we understood our true nature and what we had to do in those ancient times. We bring our story forth to share the beliefs in that day that still linger on in your day.

Honi, honi, honi. We bring forth our ideas of creation that were given us by the Manchu tribes, those people who had a penchant for speaking in another worldly form. They made many sounds unfamiliar to us, but we understood that they were communicating to a force unseen and unheard by us. We watched in wonder at these people, and how they went about their daily routines and customs. They let us in on their secret in their communications. Their throat vibrations let out a screeching sound and the air around them changed. They were a mystical people, and we learned much through our observations of them.

It became obvious to us that they formed a tribe unlike all other tribes on the earth. Their communications brought them their needs. If they wanted rain, then they manifested rain. If they wanted foods from the forest grounds, they exhibited their fortitude in developing large edible plants that would sustain them for weeks without the need for other food consumption. They knew how to tame the forces of the gods on this earth. They had no need for fear as the wild animals were their friends. They worked with the unseen and unheard forces of life. They blended with those forces, thus they were able to manifest whatever they needed for their embodiment upon earth.

Our tribe, known as the Zealots, was raised by our ancestors and we succumbed to nature, not knowing that we could manipulate these forces. At first we watched with wonder how the Manchu lived. Then we understood their make-up knowing that their abilities were available to all living beings. Because we were raised thinking we were on earth to survive the forces, it took us a long time to realize our potential. The Manchu tribe accepted us as their students demonstrating their abilities. We learned in baby steps these abilities. Each step we took totally amazed and fascinated us. Even though we could not reach their abilities, we continued their stories. The Manchu tribe eventually left the earth so they could continue and grow in their adeptness at creation.

We wish to share some of their stories and how they lived. They lived in aggregates of ten women and ten men. Their offspring were raised in a separate compound after their first three to six months of life, depending upon their suckling practices. Most of the men and women paired themselves as "married" couples, but this practice was of their choosing. Their children then lived in quarters that nurtured them mentally, physically, and spiritually. Emotionally, they all were well-rounded happy children. They did not understand fear, anger, and hate. This was not part of their people. They were taught in schools, mostly by the hands-on approach. They sat in meditation for up to two hours a day, then shared their visions with the other children and their mentors. These visions taught them that other cultures exist in other realms, and they could chose what they wanted to experience. They experimented with their visions in their schools. Many children had very similar experiences, and this assisted them in their experiments. They knew their abilities, yet they still needed to practice in producing their intended manifestations. At the age of ten, the children moved on into another compound where they could work in labs. These labs were not the scientific labs that you have today, but were labs that worked with the soils and plants of their location. They did have the ability to genetically alter their plants to balance their physical needs. They had tremendous mind power. Their power source was their minds coupled with that of the earth. They could feel the earth's power, the electromagnetic energy that runs through the veins of earth. They could harness this power into light, accelerated growth of the plant kingdoms, as well as repair their own bodies when the need arose. When the children became of age, fifteen, they went on to work the forests. They also went into the rock quarries with their amazing abilities of stone cutting and shaping. They built magnificent yet simple edifices. They excelled in sports and congregated with others their own age as teenagers do today. Upon turning age twenty, they started their own groups of ten women and ten men. These groups did specific tasks that they assigned to themselves. The groups interacted with one another along with the children. They had their "theaters" and enjoyed playfully mocking various types of birds. They held a deep reverence for all birds, thus their actors had elaborate bird-like costumes.

 The elders merged their groups as ones in their group made their transitions into another space and time. Most of them left their bodies at will, and they lived many hundreds of years if that is what they desired. Most of them decided that a life of about 150 to 200 years was enough time for a life on the earth. Of course, many decided to reincarnate into a new body and returned to their former tribe. In their new body, they continued their recognition of the tribe.

We, the Zealots, know what is possible on this earth and started to live a similar life. Born into us were memories of our ancestors that were hard to bury. Thus we could not make our lives like the Manchu tribes, but we learned so much from them. We share with you this story about these magnificent peoples and know that this earth shall return in another time to bring back this same magnificence to all people that want to be a part of this world.

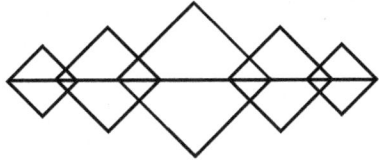

Q – Are The Zealots the same people that were a Jewish political movement in the First Century?
A – The Zealots you are referring to, those who are named in your Holy Bible, are a different tribe of people. Their teachings (those in your Bible) came from the writings and stories told them by a group of "gods" who came from the skies, the Anunnaki. The Zealots in this writing were a small civilization who migrated to the shores of southern Asia.

Q – There is a tribe called Manchu who are from Cambodia. Is the Manchu tribe in this writing have any relation to these Manchu people who live today?
A – Yes and no. The Manchu people that live today took the name of this now defunct tribe that is discussed in this writing.

Q – Why is this writing titled "A Clear Expression of You"?
A – You are a clear expression of your higher self or godself. These people, the Manchu, had and lived that knowledge. You, too, will soon be living breathing this clear expression of you. Expression refers to experiencing.

June 26, 2008

The Mystery of Avalon

The story of Avalon has been passed down through many generations and there now is talk if this place ever existed. This next book will describe this place and, indeed, Avalon exists and has existed for many millennia.

What is it that man continues to want to live in utopia when utopia is only their choice? Why is it that man continues to wrest and writhe over unseen momentum that is their choice? Then how does man perceive himself to be?

As you have learned, your life is your choice and only your choice. The actions or inaction that you choose is your responsibility and no one else's. So why does man not live in a utopia? Man has yet to perceive himself the controller of his own destiny. Each lifetime has its own destiny, and this lifetime is no different than any other in that you have created your own set of circumstances. By this we mean that you create your own schedules, your likes and dislikes, your family, your friends, where you want to live, and how you want to proceed in this life. This is all in the name of soul progression.

Yes, Avalon is alive and well. Do you wish to move to such a place? Each and every one of you can do just that. Avalon, your utopia is just a thought away. Once you have cleared the emotional baggage that you have carried around and around, from lifetime to lifetime, then you can step into this new world. How do you want your new world to be? Write them down, then in a few days go back over your list, revise them if you wish. Then a few days after that, go over your revised list again, then revise again. This list is unending because you are making your living each moment by moment. You continue to create each moment. Now move the elixir of love into each continuing moment, no judgements attached. Can you feel that inner love vibrating throughout your whole body? Using love, unconditional love in all you think, do, and create, then each moment is magnificent. It can be no other way because it is YOUR creation, your Avalon of life.

The legend of King Arthur and the Round Table is a story that has been told time and time again. It is life moving in a circle until that circle is complete in love. Did Arthur exist? Yes, he lived on the Emerald Isle that place of servitude to the Father, the Source that you are. He fought for the independence of the inner mind, that creative peace and piece that dwells within. In the outer world he brought the forces, the battling peoples, to lay down their arms in reverence to the Father. At that time, the Father was known as an atypical figure, much as God is perceived today. Arthur taught man to respect all man, regardless of one's stage in life. The Round Table is that symbol of life and love. As love circles, it touches all of man until man is engulfed in that frequency. Did Arthur marry his sister? He did in that all of man is related within this sphere. He did not marry his biological sister, but felt the ambiguity that was laid before him. He knew not of his status until the temptation of his man-ness was challenged. He knew of himself as one who would lead his countrymen to the forefront of their liberty, for the countrymen to decide for themselves their own reasons to live the life that they choose. The female man of that day knew what they had to do in order for the male of man to release their judgments of superior over inferior ideas of the sexes. The female helped teach the system of equality (a regret of religion) only to tell their tale of sacrifice in the name of the holy one of Life. They sacrificed no more and brought their power to eliminate the crevice between man and woman.

The mists of Avalon detailed the veil of forgetfulness that man was experiencing in that day. The life of Morgan lifted the veil, albeit for a short time, to reveal man's insidious behavior of superiority. In the well where life began were the waters of spirit lifted into the hearts of all in the community of Avalon.

Lift up your own hearts and hear the sighs as both man and woman pour love into their life streams to continue life into the new utopia of existence. This life on Earth shall soon be the utopia of all nations, hearts intertwined. This is the New Earth.

July 10, 2008

Hear the Chalice of Your Words

It was deemed long ago that words, expressions of thought, will be the new way of communication among the people or humans of this fine earth. The human was to be the catalyst of thoughts projecting into the unknown new creation. Creation is the here and now, always has been, and always will be. It just is.

To put this into simpler terms, your projections, each of you humans, are your creations, those thoughts you wish to develop into action. When "you wish upon a star, it makes no difference who you are," a phrase of one of your popular songs. So when you wish upon a star, you are projecting your thoughts. The star in the sky doesn't make your wish come true, but the star in you that makes it all happen. You are a part of the cosmos, yet you succumb to the frailties of human life on earth. Now those frailties will disappear and you will not look back. This human that you are is now moving into your rightful place in the world of form. It is not that you haven't been in your rightful place all along, but you did not consciously know this. Many of you still think that you are born into this world to work, to play, then eventually die, and maybe get to heaven if you are good enough and saved. Wow, what a misunderstanding of the real you.

The chalice that is you, come out into this wonderful world of form and drop all that foolishness you have believed in and know that you are God. This is not what many call New Age mumble jumble. Love you, love yourself the same as you love God (they are the same). So speak your truths, speak your wants, speak your desires. They are your thoughts manifesting into words and let these words reflect who you are.

Listen to you and listen carefully. Know your thoughts before you speak them into being. Know that your reality is your thoughts made manifest. In the next age of evolution, your perception of your reality will greatly change. It is in this moment that you will perceive your existence as much more than your current physical body. It is so much more and we have spoken of this many times. Soon you will get it, very soon. You are now being asked to let go of the old perceptions of being. The new (not really new) way of being will catapult you into multi-dimensions with just your thoughts, those creative thoughts. You will no longer wonder what the future holds for you because you will no longer be in that space where you will have such thoughts. Start now, and this way of being will be much easier to contain. The grandness of your being is now being shown to you and by you. With total love from God, the Source of You, will (the divine will) this plan be put into place. It has begun.

Namaste.

July 2, 2008

The Rise of the Roman Empire

The rise of the Roman Empire started back of what you consider ancient times. A series of rulers became Pharaohs, those that ruled because of their family's control over the people and their selected territories. Many of the pharaohs lived meaningful lives and ruled with the people instead of for the people. Other pharaohs did not know how to control the people because they felt it was the duty of the learned hierarchy to give them means to interpret their selfish ways. Of course, this did not work, and the ruling people rebelled. A lot of bloodshed was created, and new rulers rose up to help those they considered less fortunate, those not part of the ruling parties.

In these ancient times, the interior party is the one who controlled most of the peoples on this earth plane. They moved into place their own dynasty, their own ruling factions, of which the family of Pharaohs was a part. However, most of the Pharaohs were not aware of such control that manipulated their many moves. They felt that it was their duty to hold power over the people making up laws that were not conducive to knowledge and wisdom. Indeed, knowledge begets wisdom and this was withheld from the populace.

Now you may be wondering why this writing is included. Those that live in the inner circles understand this plan very well for their forefathers constructed this plan that even exists today. What the people on this Earth and others that exist beyond this Earth do not realize is that these members of this ruling party extend well beyond this space and time. These interdimensional beings have a saying that they truly believe in, and that saying is: "He that shall fault the dominion of thy world shall falter in his endeavors. He that lives by those laws instituted beyond this earthly realm, shall know of their presence in all worlds. Know ye and ye shall know God." The statement "Know ye and ye shall know God" may be blasphemous to many, but think of what this is saying. "Know ye" is to know yourself, even yourself in other worlds. Because of this, man on this Earth are beginning to understand their nefarious ways and returning to their god-head. To further understand what this all means is to understand the significance of the wanderer, that part of each of you that wanders through creation, viewing the possibilities, coming into contact with the other aspects of yourself that you, dear gods, have put into place so you can know yourselves.

So who has been behind the many scenarios that have played out on this Earth? Each one of you. Your Earth, this plane of existence, has given you a playground of experiences that you will not get elsewhere. Each of you have devised your very own plans that you put into place, hence practice, to know of yourself living in the experience of being human. You have raised your flag and said "I am here." You are indeed very clever at being human, that you forgot that you are God. And now you are returning to that aspect of you who remembers, who remembers that you are only part of the whole.

Remember when you fell down as a child and your mother would kiss your hurt? Well your mother is kissing your hurt, not your physical mother, but the mother inside of you, that feminine creative side of yourself. You fell down, you only think you got hurt, but you did not. Maybe a little bruised, but definitely not hurt. You have come through this plan with flying colors, each of you waving your flags. No longer do you need the advice of the external hierarchy. No longer do you truly need the governance of the external body. No longer do you need the Pharaoh's laws to protect the selfish ones of power.

Rise up, dear ones, rise up! Rise up your very own empire that you are! That strength, the Roman god and goddess, rise up through your very own plan. Beseech yourselves onto the new land, the land of plenty. Your new world is at your fingertips. Create this world from your hearts, and let your minds enter in with the force that you now may feel is impossible. In God, there is no thing that is impossible. All things are ready to explore. The possibilities become the probabilities, and the probabilities become the norm. Your new world is before you. How do you wish to create? Bring to yourself, all of you, the knowledge of life unending. Wonderful creative creatures, embrace the wisdom, embrace the catalyst that has brought you to this place and time. Release the need to control the flock. Let your wings rise into the midst of eternal love.

What is wisdom? Wisdom is knowing that you are indeed God, creating every moment with a plan emanating from the heart source. Consciously demand your inner essence to release the past and forgive yourself. Despair will never again be a part of you. Let yourself go into your heart and live from that very essence. Your world is changing like the flip of a switch. Turn on your lights, let them shine brightly and your world will be vastly different than it is today. How do you want to be in this new world? It is totally up to you, grand creator. Let go of your perceived past, those transgressions that brought you to this place and time. Know they are your past and you would not be "here" if it wasn't for this past. Love it, honor it, then let it go.

We hear that many people do not know how to act in this present world, and therefore, have no clue how to create their new world. To start, stop relying on the pharaoh's, those you think govern you. Stop relying on those false notions that say you are not good enough, not good enough for what? Stop relying on those family members you think validate yourself. Each of you are valid individuals, otherwise you would not be here. Take responsibility for everything in your life, every thought, every action, or non-action. You embodied on this earth plane, so make the most of it. Love each minute of your existence here on earth. When doing this, your existence will, indeed, change. This sounds so simple, yet most on earth do not know this. Knowledge begets wisdom. Allow those feelings of peace wash over and through your bodies. Let them enter into every cell of your being. Stay in this peace and your earth will be a new place.

So be it, and it is so.

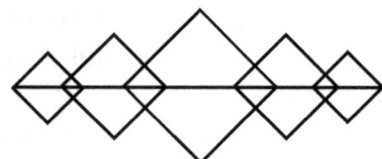

Q – Why is this book titled "The Rise of the Roman Empire?"
A – The Roman gods and goddesses that all of humanity embrace stands for strength and perseverance. Hence, you all have persevered through your many lifetimes on this earth, and now use that inner strength to rise into the whole of yourselves.

Q – Are you saying that the word "Roman" implies strength?
A – The title "Roman" comes from the word romance or "from the heart." Strength, indeed, comes from the heart.

Q – This book says that the rulers of the ancient Roman Empire were called Pharaohs. I thought the title Pharaohs were those kings who ruled Egypt, not Rome. Please explain.

A – In ancient days, the rulers of large sects of land and people were called kings and another word for king is pharaoh, a ruling family. Ruling families felt that they were the ones who were put into power by the gods. Those from other realms (extraterrestrials) were deemed gods because they came from the skies or heavens.

July 21, 2008

The Rumblings

It is clear that this time called science of the divine is a clear indication of your ability to transcend the consciousness of your perceived third dimension. As you continue along in your understandings of knowledge and wisdom, will you understand the complexities of mass consciousness that radiates on the plane of physical existence, the overlying matrix of consciousness you see as your world. Everyone's world is a little bit different, as each sees with their own set of eyes, not only their physical eyes, also the other eyes that are within them. Remember when you created in the time track you developed with the knowledge your forebear's brought with them, you in another time and place, so to speak? It is the mountains that you have moved. It is the rivers that you have maneuvered as you rode the currents of the hour. Now that is about to change. In fact, it has changed but you are not yet aware of all of these changes.

Now is the moment to speak your truths of divine being. To go out and beat your chests saying I know the way, I have the light, and follow me will not bring anyone to your side. Instead when you speak your truths that you are love incarnate and that love shows through your words and actions, will you get another's attention. That, indeed, is heaven on earth. It is the rapture, the ascension many of you have been talking about. Many beings have felt that this rapture is where you will lift off of this earth into a grand heaven. Some of you will do just that. All of you have that capability, however, each of you have incarnated on this earth for a reason. And that reason is to know yourself. That's all, just know yourself. Huh? Whisper these words "the Lord is thy shepherd and I shall not want. He maketh me lie down in green pastures. He restoreth my soul." So now you are living on this beautiful blue-green earth, lying down in the green pastures, understanding that you are divine.

Beautiful humans, you are restoring your souls, bringing into this world more aspects of the divine. You understand your own uniqueness and that cannot be taken away. You live by the golden rule of love for your brother as well as yourselves. This is the rumblings, the rumblings within your very soul.

As you continue on your way of light and truth, you will know there is no thing that is impossible. Your abilities will outnumber any of the limitations of your doing. Do you understand what this means? You will outnumber even all of your dreams that you now hold. You will do what is now perceived as the impossible. I can name a few of these for you, to start stretching your minds into unlimited thinking and creating.

1. Transchanneling. Your ability to "speak" in the language of light, that is in symbols and numbers. This ability will assist you to understand many other species that reside off of this earth.
2. Understand and use new technologies that include bio-location, being in more than one location simultaneously and being conscious of doing so.
3. Waking your subconscious and knowing all of your past lives and integrating these experiences into your present reality.
4. Time travel
5. Interplanetary travel

6. Working with the elements of this earth to present a new way of living biologically. The growth of your foods will not only be through your soils, but with hydroponics, something you are experimenting with now.
7. Air extraction. Your ability to extract your oxygen and hydrogen for clean air to breathe, a new technology that is already in the works! This is through your labs. You will continue to use plant life as an exchange of elements, but you will have the addition of a new technology that includes mechanically producing depollinated currents containing water to balance your eco systems.
8. Harness electricity with the use of your oceans.
9. Oil will not be used to motor your vehicles. Your vehicles will be powered by the use of magnetics and cross currents (interplay of electromagnetic energy).
10. The past can change the future. So in your time travels, you will be unable to change the course that you already have set before you. Therefore, no fear will be realized. All fear will fade from your existence.

It is through your will that all will be made new. It has been spoken by you and for you. So it is!

September 16, 2008

Cross Walks

In the boldness of standing in your holy presence, ask yourself the following questions. These are just a tease to where you as human beings are going as you traverse your states of physical being into higher states of consciousness into the new worlds of Matter.

In the compass of the new world you will find that the means to exist will have shifted greatly. Your means of survival will shift. What once was very important to you will cease to be. What shall become of this new human, you in the human flesh of gods creating the next generation of biological bodies? What is it that makes you "tick" and want to bring a whole new being-ness to yourselves? Indeed, what have each one of you devised for yourself? It is you creating your present, and nothing "out there" (there really is no thing out there) will hold you back. Even the ships in the skies that will become quite prevalent in the days to come will have no influence over you. You will work (create) together in this mass of consciousness.

The matrix that now surrounds your wonderful planet, Earth, is now in place and will give you the tools to take evolutionary jumps into the dimensions foretold to you. What you will see, produce, expand upon into the next phases of life within life will catapult you to new understandings of the many forces of life, unending, into the foreverness of All That

Is. What are the new tools that you will need to get to this place of understanding? It is You in your own consciousness of understanding the full You, in all its grandeur.

You are now learning what it means to be a creator. The laws of attraction have been spoken and are being consciously utilized. The universe that responds to your requests is energy following energy. It is the combination of your thoughts that generate these thoughts as energy that brings to you what you desire. If you feel it is not what you desire, just change your thoughts. It is as simple as that. What you truly desire is what you manifest, it can be no other way. You have heard the saying "be careful what you wish for" not really understanding how this manifestation works. You may say: "God knows what I want and need. He will only give me what I can handle, nothing more." Or you may say: "I surrender to God's will." Do you truly understand what surrendering to God's will really means?

You are that God you surrender to. It is you and if you do not want to give yourself more than you feel you can handle, then don't challenge yourself to that degree. We, on this side of the veil, see what happens when you do not reach your self-made goals. You feel guilty. And what kind of energy is guilt? It pulls you down, and then builds upon itself. Ask yourself if that is the way you want to live your life. You, as the human beings on the Earth, have devised the duality program and now you know how that works. Now another part of yourself is planning the changes that are now taking place upon the earth plane of existence. Listen to the big You. It is You, God, talking. It is the You of your internal being wanting out of the sacred vessel into a more realized vessel of love and understanding. You are always sacred because you are God. You are splendor and now desire a more harmonious life.

Listen. Listen to your internal strength. You know what you must do to live harmoniously. Start creating your every day with your hearts wide open. The heart connects you to Source, the source of your total being. Anything that you give energy to that disrupts this process will bring to you what you really do not want. Always be kind to yourself. Any self-deprecation can be hazardous to your health, mental and physical.

A new day dawns. Create your lives in balance of the divine, both the masculine and the feminine, the right and left hemispheres of your brain in tune with the recorder of your hearts. Yes, a new day dawns. It is here, in the now. Listen with divine intent of love understanding love. Love thyself and see thyself in all eyes you come in contact with.

The future is in front of you yet you cannot get there until you live in the present. The many factions of yourselves will come into view and you will know what you must do. It is in the balance of all you do, say, and think. You are now crossing those lines, the lines within the matrix of love and understanding, the matrix of this universe as it connects to other matrices of other universes. You will know, you will see, and you will understand just how grand it is to be human.

With much gratitude, we extend our hearts to you in this grand process that is now taking place on this earth, in this earth, that extends beyond this earth, into your solar system, then reaches out and touches the absolute ALL.

We are the Grand Masters, in accordance to the mandate that love only exists in the new universe.

October 1, 2008

The Car Salesman

An unusual title, don't you think? Let us take a look at your marketplace where you buy and sell goods. First you have a reason for the goods to be made. What determines those reasons? All of mankind, your animals, and even your plant kingdom have what you call the survival instinct. In order for each of you to survive on this earth plane, you need food, water, and some kind of shelter. For you to survive emotionally, you need love, the kind of love given with no expectations, just the warm embrace or touch of one for another. It is a basic human need. As you have learned in the first volume of "Mystery of the Universes," there is a science of the divine. Your basic thoughts become your reality, and for those thoughts to manifest themselves, you have a transference of energy, not only within your physical body, but the energy surrounding your body and the matrix you have built that connects you to everyone else on earth and beyond.

October 7, 2008

We shall continue this message knowing that your current marketplace is making huge changes. And why is this happening? It is because the base that was your marketplace is crumbling. And it is crumbling because the energies that upheld it are no longer in place. Your world has moved past the need to train the population that the more you put on your plate, the better. It has been a constant "doing" for those caught up in the world of materialism. To have material goods is absolutely fine, however, people, those in the more civilized countries, are beginning to realize what is important to them. They are finding that just the need of "having" no longer fulfills them, it never did. They are taking on a new perspective of what it means to survive on this earth. They are starting to question their very existence. Some of you questioned your existence many years ago. You read the books, wrote in your journals, trying to understand God. And now you know that your existence is much more than you ever thought or comprehended. We still say, your existence is so much more than you will ever comprehend, here on this 3rd plane of existence.

The reality of what we are sharing with you is that your current way of buying and selling goods will drastically change. It is like your car salesman. The customers walk in the showrooms or onto your car lots and see the bounty of powerful shiny cars that are homes on wheels. A salesman approaches you and asks if he or she can be of assistance. You ponder if you even want to share that drive within you that you really would like to purchase a shiny new car. You like the feel of a new car, the way it handles, the amount of room inside its shell, and the overall feeling of "look at me" as you envision yourself driving a new vehicle. Have you ever pondered as to what gives you this feeling of want and need? The salesman's job is to fulfill that want and need. They are there to service that part of you called ego, but is there a deeper level of manifestation that is occurring? A good salesman will tap into that knowledge, that deeper level within you. He or she will notice that insecurity within you. They will take that insecurity and help you understand that a shiny new car is what you need to be secure. The car is new, it is a trusted brand, it is warranted, and it is safer than the old car you are driving.

Can you see how this works? Each of you is that car salesman. You are taking those old insecurities, moving them out of your existence. You are making a shiny new life for yourselves. You soon will be trusting everything you think and do. How is this happening? You are tapping into the power of You, that awesome power of You many of you call God.

All of those industries, corporations, even small companies that are solely in place for you to discern what is for your highest good will be as a beacon to new understandings. Those companies that tell you that you need something you are not comfortable with will soon go out of business. Those companies that manufacture goods and services that assist you and Lady Gaia, your Earth, are the ones who will be honored for their presence. They are honored because they provide your needs.

Let us take a look at your needs. Everyone's needs are not the same. Remember that you are here on this earth to experience, to learn lessons, to grow in your spirit of understanding you. Even though you are much grander than this one life, this one life that you are now living in this now moment, this life is the one you nourish. That is your job, only yours. You each volunteered to be here now, in this moment. So what are your needs? To sustain the body, you need food that nourishes every part of your body. To sustain your emotional body, you need love to keep you in balance. It is your job to receive and recognize this love, not get it outside of yourself. It is in you, the very heart of your being, the God within you. Perhaps it is better to say, feel what already is a part of yourself. To sustain your mental body, know that you exist to enjoy the fruits of your thoughts. You live with what you create.

To further understand your needs, know that you are here to create. Those goods and services that you create on this earth plane are ones that nourish your soul, the you within You. Your soul encompasses your full bodies – physical, emotional, and mental. It is you, the spirit, that has chosen those bodies. You are now remembering, becoming conscious of why you are here. Therefore your needs are changing. Let us take a look at some of those changes in your goods and services sector.

- Companies will manufacture only those goods that enhance your consciousness. Clothes will continue as art. Not only are clothes to protect your physical selves, but also reflect your personality. Clothes will also feed your needs in the moment. Some days you will need the color red to bring in more love and activity. Other days, you feel more contemplative and you will feel like wearing blue. Clothes and shoes that are uncomfortable and play against the naturalism of your body will be phased out because people will discontinue purchasing them. The tie for men, the high heels for women are two such items.
- Foods and their production will increasingly be done through the process of enclosed ponics. To protect foods from the ravishes of your earth's birthing, i.e. storms, your foods, fruits and vegetables will be grown on large lots of land in multiple level greenhouse type structures. In development are ways of naturally producing organic foods in controlled environments. Also, many more households will grow their own fruits and vegetables in the gardens next to their homes or in lots that are shared with others. There will always be plenty of food to feed everyone on this earth. For everyone to eat properly, there will be a need for teachers of agriculture to go out and teach the people how to do this. Some foods will continue to be genetically engineered and this will not produce less effective or nutritional varieties. The eating of your meats will decline with your new foods producing the necessary vitamins, minerals, and proteins that will sustain the body in its fullest capacity.

- Arts. The arts will continue to be important in your societies. They not only teach through the performing arts but also through the arts of drawing, painting, and pottery making. All art tells a story and this is a way for people to express themselves. It also gives beauty to life, an important ingredient.

The coming events that you will see on this earth are varied and will bring humanity into another state of evolution. It has already started and will escalate as humanity refocuses their thoughts into new manifestations.

Be as the car salesman. The shiny new vehicle is you.

November 4, 2008

Trees in the Forest

Many trees make up a forest. There may be thousands of different species of trees all in one forest. Add to the trees, you will find thousands of bushes, small plants, an array of rocks and minerals that bring more magnificence to a forest. Bring in the many animals who receive their nourishment from the forest, and vice versa, the many plants and trees receive their nourishment from the animals as well as the earth, sun, and water. What a conundrum of activities that go on every moment of every day. It is life growing and responding to one another. It is life building then decaying, bringing new life at every turn. What a wonderful world you have built. Many of you say that God built this earth and you would be correct. Know that all is God and it always is in the making. Your earth continues to be made new. What has gone on before what you call past time no longer exists. It cannot exist because only this moment exists. Did the trees, plants, animals exist in the past? They certainly did, but they are now made new.

    Can you now understand how life works? Every moment is a new moment begotten of new energy released from the Creator energy. You are that creator creating every moment with every thought that you create. It is energy changing, morphing, always new. It is bursts of light emanating from the thoughts and the dreams of creators. It is the fulcrum of activity, releasing, renewing, breathing life into form. It is the totality of thoughts made manifest into the dream world you continue to create. It is both the magnificent and the magnificence. What appears new is thoughts rearranging themselves. It is energy moving in such a fashion to evoke the spoken word, the written word, the song of songs. It is the movement of songs (or sound) in the here and now of this world and all other worlds. You touch all. Your voice rises into the heavens of all worlds. Your song plays upon itself. The incredible works are God made manifest. It is such a feat!

Every leaf upon the many trees in the forest is an individual manifestation. Within the leaf is a pulsing of song or light. It is energy moving, making new every moment, one upon the next. This process of light, energy moving into form, is the light of Creator Source, the Source of All. It does not judge, it does not falter, it just is. The ebb and flow of energy is made possible through the development of zanambiism, the likeness not unlike the stillness within each and every one of mankind. It is the power that each one of you hold within. It is the Creator's energy emanating through His creations, you. It is the power, the glory, forever and ever. Create in gladness and you will find interesting ideas that lift all of creation. It is and ever shall be. The seed of life grows, becomes new, moment upon moment. The new mankind shall not and will not ever falter. The new creations are upon this earth. The new way of being is here and always has been "here," and you are now realizing this truth. You are realizing the truth of what it means to be human. You are realizing what it means to be God in the flesh. There are no dictums that you must follow. The only laws are the universal laws of love and this love can be broken down into many parts. All is wrapped up in the cloak of continuous life, unending, eternal. The new physics, what is termed new but always is, is your ability to see this unending spiral of creation. You can see this in the leaf, attached to the tree, attached to the earth, attached to this system of light, all within the Great One.

There are trees in the forest. Animals roam these forests and live in them. The rocks and minerals are there to supply added life to the trees, to the leaves, and to the animals. Life is unending. It begins every moment, building, dividing, building, dividing, then implodes upon itself and starts again. These grand cycles you have developed enable you to see or realize the grandness of just being. The source of you and All That Is just Is.

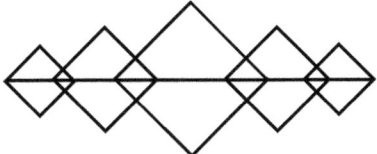

Q – In paragraph there is the word "zanambiism." I do not find this word in our dictionary. This writing says the ebb and flow of energy is made possible through this development, similar to the stillness within us. Please further explain this word.

A – Yes, we come up with "new" words when giving you these writings and truths. This word "zanambiism" is from the root word "zanabi," a culture who has existed on this Earth plane, and lived a most serene life. They were much like your Tibetan monks who spend much of their time in a meditative state.

January 13, 2009

The Promise

In this eleventh hour of change, humanity is much in a panic. What is happening on this earth plane is the movement that started two ages ago in the "time" of the metamorphosis of the one known as man. Man, indeed, has evolved, not from monkeys, for they are another species, a distant cousin to the humans. But man has transformed itself into a more realized body of light. This is in agreement to what the higher beings of light called the Airophim, the Nephilim, and the overseers, the Elohim, have promised. They have put into place the new seed of consciousness to override the planet of duality, known as Earth.

This wake-up call has been super-seeded into a whole new paradigm of understanding and willingness to experience life in another fashion. What is happening on the plane of third-dimensional earth is the movement of the Earth's most basic inner form, and that is the release of quantum particles that made up the inner sanctums of this planet. The inner core of the planet has indeed gone through a metamorphosis. The inner light, or crystalline structure that is the heart of earth, a physical incarnation of the Being known as Gaia, is changing to meet the needs of Gaia as well as man who resides on her outer surface. Those beings that live on her interior have been the fornicators of this transition. They have used their abilities to bring added light, the transmutation of form, into a focus of recognized abundance of photon particles articulating into a form that appears or is recognized as the christed light. This light is the formation of the particles that wave in patterns not known on the earth plane. What man will be witnessing is the intersection of the wave particles that produce a new light or color to the eyes of man. It is an iridescence or colors that are familiar yet leave a radiance, a bleed through of light through color. It gives a shimmering effect.

Man, in his ability to see through his eyes and his inner eye, will be able to focus on this shimmering light and see new forms take shape. These forms are the thoughts of man entering into the new way of manifestation. Form will take shape right before their eyes! This is the new alchemical process taking place. It is the way of manifestation that is known as the golden era. Man, indeed, will be living a new way of life. His world will look vastly different as this process comes into being. Thought, change of thought from that of duality, will be in the beauty of form formed through the higher vibrations originating through the heart chakra. As these news forms emerge, the old forms of fear, distrust, apathy, and so-called evil will fall away. It will be a most wondrous transformation. It is in process, and this process will continue until it takes hold on this earthen plane. Many blessings to you all who witness this transformation. You are the seeds into this new plan of love manifesting through your very own hearts.

December 28, 2008

Now and Forever More

On this day humanity shall be the ones who shall bring all forces into the One. They shall stir the masses until the pot has boiled over. Then they shall look into the pot and see what is left. This, dear ones, is what humanity is doing at this most auspicious time. What is left in the pot is the base of each one of you. It is your soul showing itself in all of its glory. It is the god or creator within each one of you that is calling forth to be recognized for what it is, for what each one of you are.

These times that you call The End Times are indeed the end times. It is you shedding those costumes that you adorned so you would hide from yourself. We call that pretty creative! Those costumes shall vanish and not return for you have no need of these anymore.

Do you humans want to know your past, how you reached this period of time that you call ascension? Each one of you has lived a multitude of lives. Most of these lives were lived on this beautiful green and blue planet you call earth. This earth is so much grander as it spins its way into the new era, the new space that is called eternal. As the earth sheds its coat, all of humanity will recognize the beautiful being that resides in the skin and core of this most wonderful body. The earth, our dear Lady

Gaia, shall speak to each and every one of you that live in and on her surface. She is saying that she shall be treated with respect and with grace. Her powers are beyond a human's means and she has the power to reproduce at will and she often does. Why do humans not notice these abilities? Your costumes have even covered your eyes and ears. All things go on before your eyes yet you do not see them. They are measurable. You currently have instruments that can measure such things and they are called your tuning devices. The tune or vibration of this earth changes constantly and when you are in tune with the earth, then you can perceive these changes.

The earth's power source, the internal chamber, receives and sends out vibrations that tell others within the universe, and indeed universes (the many dimensions), that it is alive. When the earth does not feel well or its tune is out of kilter, then the signal is received by other like bodies, and the signals are sent back to the earth's core to assist in the harmony of the sphere, the body that you stand on. There are many who assist this earth in this manner. They are here by the hundreds of thousands. By here we mean that they reside in the atmospheres of this earth, outside the atmospheres, as well as within the body of earth. This experiment forming the duality to bring the forces together has been an extraordinary accomplishment. It is not quite finished but the end time draws near. Those of you who have chosen to be here now are a witness to this grand event. It is all of you who planned it. Let what remains unfold and be released. Let this plan be finished. It is time to move forward into a new life, a new time, a new plan. The next few years shall be wondrous! What happens may not be what you consciously expect. The tears shall dry up. Tears, a releasing tool, are there for each one of you to experience. Then the tears shall turn to laughter and praise that you, every one of you, have done it! You have shed your costumes.

January 28, 2009

The Night Rider

The energy of this writing shall be felt within all who read it. It is a template for the higher visions to manifest on this earthen plane of physical existence. Peace and love to all who shall enter this doorway. What you will see, hear, and feel shall be a new experience for many of you. Enjoy the ride into the newer dimensions of physicality. You are at the steering wheel yet when you combine with thoughts of your Higher Self you shall travel to new heavens. Peace along your roads as you see your visions form right before your eyes. Namaste.

    Come into this realm of beauty, quietude, and seemingly endless visions stretching out before you. See the myriad forms of energy take shape then dissipate. Concentrate on the form you wish to see. Form in your mind the details, see them come into place or a place. As this formation appears know that it is your creation. You have the ability to change it at will, let it be, or grow with your focused intent. You, indeed, are forming new worlds. A world is not necessarily a planet, but your very own piece of space yet shared within the many dimensions. All manifestation is the here and now. It is constantly forming, then dissipating to be formed again yet in a new patterning. Holy ones of this New Age, see your world with new eyes. Have the fortitude to know that you are the lords of creation. You combine with other manifestations of Creator, aspects unbeknownst to you, yet part of the One.

Know within your Being of Beings, that it is You, the maker of heaven on and in this earth. It is You that has chosen to be participating with the other aspects of Creator to live in synchronicity with this Being you call Gaia.

As you visualize your current existence, see it extend into the omniverse. Let yourselves go into this void. It is a void yet are the forces of Creator allowing you to do with this energy whatever you want. Only from the energy of your heart will you be able to manifest or see the many manifestations of your brethren. So go into that place of quiet solitude and remain there, just remain there. Quiet your mind, and if you need this tool, just see the colors as they burst before your closed eyes (physical). Just stay there and watch the fireworks, one bursting with a multitude of colors, one on top of the other. Soon you will find nothing, maybe the white light as these colorful bursts are intermixed. Stay there and just be. Feel the calmness as you remain in this exalted state. Now hear the voice of god, that part of you called your Higher Self. It may sound like a masculine voice or a feminine voice, it does not matter. Stay in that space of unlimited love.

As you get comfortable with this exercise, you will be able to move mountains. Your inner world will become your outer world and all of your worlds shall be One. Understand one another and allow your manifestations to work together. Know that all manifestations, your creations, come from the heart of God. You are now that heart and Know that It Is So.

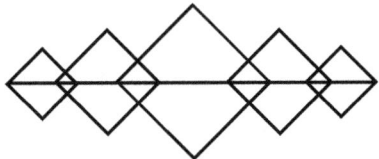

Q – Please explain why this writing is called "Night Rider."
A – Rider is self-explanatory when you read the message. The

word "night" implies the dream state, that state you create in. And this state does not mean when you are asleep. It is when you dream through your visions, those wants and desires that manifest themselves. Through the darkness, you see light. And this light glows within you and is getting stronger and stronger as your bodies allow for this to happen. Remember all is connected, all of creation.

February 6, 2009

The Chronicles[1]

It has been said that as we perform our lifetimes, we will progress in the worlds of wonder, excitement, newness, a liking to all that is and will ever be. It is the true understanding that we are the makers of heaven and earth, the rich and the poor, the beloved of beloveds. We are the stars of today, of tomorrow, of eternal life unfolding into infinite patterns of love made manifest. Until we realize our potentiality, we shall flounder in the presence. We shall flounder in the worlds of form. We shall flounder in the worlds of gods as we move along the spectrum of this potentiality.

Beings of this universe, act as though this is your last moment in time because it is your last moment in time. When you move out of the timeline, there only is. There only is potentiality. When you realize the undividedness of this all, there is only the love that can be, the love that can manifest into potentiality. Creator gods, know that you Are because you create it so. Create in gladness and know that the end result is only part of the equation of your manifestation. It is the intention behind the thoughts. It is the release of the thoughts that move the intention into form.

Beloveds, you have performed well. But there is more, a lot more. Know this, understand this. Within the all of You, see the transformation. It is in movement, always in movement.

It is up to you to move "forward" or "backward," for they are one and the same. You have built your fortresses, tore them down, built new ones. And this continues ad infinitum. Humanity is on the precipice of new understandings, new manifestations. They are making a huge leap into the abyss of the unknown. This is a most wondrous feat. The knowledge that will be gained will be unlike anything that humanity has yet to accomplish. And that is the love vibration that has turned the corner into a more realized form of being. You shall see the likeness of mankind in various forms, forms that you now cannot comprehend. That is okay, for soon you shall know, know of this new existence. Are you ready?

Just taking that leap of faith will catapult you into this new form of being. It is not radical, nor is it to be feared. In fact, there shall be no more fear for that is a manifestation of the lower man not yet ready for the kingship of being. You shall know when to take this leap. Be not afraid and you will not falter. Know within your being that this new world awaits you. You will tie in many of the other aspects of your Whole Being. What marvelous creators you all are. You have lived, have traveled near and afar only to realize that you haven't moved at all but only in the knowing, the outward manifestation of your very own thoughts.

The stars of today and tomorrow, it makes no difference. They are only an extension of all of you creators. They are creations themselves, not separate, only a part of you. Yes, new worlds await you. You create in every aspect of Yourself and these aspects are combining to form a more realized You. Such an exciting Moment. Take that leap of faith and know that you shall land on terra firma.

We request only one thing as we share these thoughts with you. You have lived many, many lives and you have lived them well. You have made a turn around in the world of form. You have developed the need to move beyond the passion of understanding into the more visible aspect of creating wisely. You have moved into the next paradigm, into the worlds of the formless, yet you hold those codes to manifesting new forms to play in. Play well my friends, my gods of everlasting life. We join you in this new endeavor. Let us play together.

We are the gods and goddesses. You know us as the thoughts behind your thoughts. We are the spark that you feel. We are You and you are Us.

---

1 Per the dictionary: Chronicle – a usually detailed record of facts or events set down in the order of time with no attempt made to evaluate or interpret.

February 23, 2009

The Release

Clearly do we see the changes that are taking place on your beautiful planet call Gaia's Earth. It is just an explosion of color and sound that is almost deafening to the ears yet a soft whisper within the whole of creation. Your planet is drastically changing and you are beginning to see it within yourselves and earth as well as in your skies. What you are witnessing is the transformation of the Earth into the realized body of potential Stardom. It is the star in the making. Gaia is learning the truth of herself, a magnetized being of light shining her brilliance in the skies. Her time here is slowly coming to an end as she migrates to a new place in this cosmos of creation. She is making herself a conduit of light, not only the spectrum of the seven light rays, but adding the spectrum of multi-dimensionality, a pass into the higher realms of existence. She shall take her place in the frequencies of the 5th dimension and higher. Her brothers and sisters, those planets who are trekking with her, are making their own changes to fit the higher vibrations for their own evolvement. They take with them many life forms, the life form of human or humanoid, a key to their evolvement.

Within this era of change, the planets and stars involved in this process shall take their place as keys to new adventures within this creation Kingdome. This dome is built for new understandings as life takes on another garb, a new perspective.

Who built this wonderful planet called Gaia's Earth shall remove their masks to reveal themselves as the makers or coalescers of matter. This project now complete shall take another turn. It has been determined man shall be the ones who move this to another place and time sequence unlike the previous cycles of creation in this sector. Throughout this transition, man shall release all that he "thinks" he knows, for the rules or ways of manifestation are changing. It really is not a rule at all but a new process in sub-quantum physics, a new reality not yet known. The necessary arrangements are being made on a cosmic level to ensure that this process unfolds in a gentle manner so not to harm the energetic bridge that is now in place. It is taking place in the here and now and shall commence once the energetic envelop is in place. It is referred as the Third Earth.

The existing systems on Earth including the electrical systems, magnetic systems, and subatomic particle systems are morphing, or in effect closing down. Man will witness a change in everything they thought as truth. A true description cannot be made with the current criteria in physics or physical makeup. It is a whole new spectrum of creation.

We just ask for all on Earth at this time to be patient, to be observant, to be loving with themselves as well as with all others. That is the only energy that can transport into this new life. All other life will simply cease to be or appear to have ceased. The lower life forms will continue on in the lower three dimensions until such a moment that they are ready to transcend. Mankind, keep your hearts, eyes, and ears open to this most amazing and wonderful transformation.

February 28, 2009

The Truth, the Tempest, the Witch

Many, many years ago, there existed a man who wanted to experience just being a thorn in the sides of all he contacted. What bothers one person and not the next, he wondered? What makes people think and do, all of us different? As the man pondered these questions, he decided to start an experiment reading the daily ties of the people in the town in which he lived. He gathered his information just by watching the townspeople go to and fro in this small town. He even noticed the reactions in the horses during conflicts of their masters. He wondered, what excites one person and not the next? What makes them react differently to the same problem?

So in this man's daily exercises, he took in what he observed in the local vernacular. He sorted out his own beliefs, at least as much as he was able. For he knew that his own beliefs are different than the townspeople. Some of the people drew around the local bar and restaurant telling their tales of woe or excitement of their home life which, in most instances, involved a farm. Other people spent their time in the local Church of Good Faith, to which it was referred. They planned suppers, festivals, children's events, as well as community prayer all in the name of righteousness, the belief that God is the ever-seeing power that towers over them. They also talked about being in a grave, the underground life of sin, place of torture, and sadness that doomed them for eternity. They pointed many fingers at their neighbors who frequented the bar. Spirits, they believed, was a drink of hell, fire, and brimstone because it caused sickness. The other townspeople mostly stayed to themselves and their families, working off the land for their sustenance. They seemed at peace with this arrangement.

During an argument over land, one of the townspeople argued that his land was being ruined by the local band of "pet" dogs owned by a small community of church goers. The dogs were scaring the farmer's animals, causing disruption in their reproductive processes and the giving of milk by the cows. Tempers flared between the farmer and the dogs' owners. The dogs were protective of the small community but went beyond their bounds into the nearby farm. The dogs' owners simply said that the dogs were doing what dogs do and that they held no responsibility over them. The farmer disagreed. And so the development of land rights.

One of the townsmen, who had seized the property of his fellow neighbor, decided to act upon the situation that he felt would benefit the town, removing restrictions that were included in the local laws of the town. He felt it was his duty to do so overriding anyone's suggestions and recommendations on how to handle this situation. Using his own interpretation of law, he decided that all land would reside in the ownership of the whole town. Boundaries, therefore, were not enforced. This would end the problem with the dogs infringing upon the animal produce from the nearby farm.

The local townspeople rebelled and said that this idea is not fair. Why should they give up their rights to the land they so lovingly toiled for growth of foods for their families? The man would not hear of it. He felt that any foods grown on the lands were to be shared and anyone who wanted their share had a right to go onto the land and get it.

This program worked for over three years with the townspeople sharing their crops and the use of their animals until one day a new family came into town. This family saw what was going on in this community and wondered how this system of equal sharing worked. They noticed that the man who became the town's mayor (the man who set up this program) started running the town like a dictatorship, barking out new rules and regulations on this shared program. He noticed that the people who did the most toiling in the fields were rewarded with an assemblage built upon the resources of the nearby countryside. What bothered this new family the most is the resilience of the townspeople as they adjusted to this program. In the coming days the new family suggested that the town have a community meeting to discuss the whereabouts of the portions of the estates or property that once was a part of the community. They noticed that the town was being built into elaborate communal living arrangements. The town was designed around a central park, a place for the children to play yet be under watchful eyes of their parents. The work places where there existed small manufacturing processes such as horseshoe metal making were built away from the center of town. The mercantiles were built close to the homes and some were temporary stands set up near the park. The schools were open, classes in the park and families working together on the farms and in the shops. This whole set-up seemed to work quite well unless a disgruntled family felt that their toiling was being hindered by those who did not wish to contribute as much as they.

So the town meeting took place where the people voiced their concerns that all was not equal. Those families whose lives appeared to be more at peace with their ease of living were questioned by those who created unrest because of their protection of their own labor or lack thereof. They questioned the ability of those who worked together for the good of the whole versus the good of themselves. They felt such a dichotomy existed. They did not recognize their own inability to be a part of the whole "project" as it was called. Those on the outskirts of town, those farms who fed the community, started holding back on their production of foods to make their point that they felt superior because they were the food makers. They felt their foods were the town's survival products, and they were correct. However the body needs much more than foods to nourish it. One man named Butch held his own meetings in his hamlet. Many townspeople listened to Butch as he expressed that life is much more than the eating of foods, that there was a much deeper meaning to life then even the church spoke about. He said that life is beyond the mere human form. Of course, food stuffs were important, but that truly living life was much more complex. And that complexity was living a simple still life. By "still," Butch spoke about the reasons for being the physical body. He understood the deeper meaning of experiencing life. However, the townspeople rebelled against his teachings. They stripped him of his belongings to see if he could live with virtually nothing. Butch seemed to thrive with his predicament. The townspeople were astounded yet went about their business as before.

The town grew to be very large. The mayor selected his own ruling council because as the town grew, more decisions had to be made to accommodate the rapid changes going on. The townspeople began to make more of their own decisions not complying with the mayor and his council. They began again to fight for their individual rights. Most respected their neighbors, but greed started to take hold. This caused more unrest until Butch called a town meeting. Since the people knew that Butch easily survived his being an outcast decided to hear what Butch had to tell them. The townspeople met in the central park.

Butch made his entrance into the park by pulling his own wagon which contained all of his belongings. Butch stood upon his wagon and started telling the people a story. This story was about a time in which the world was at war with itself. The townspeople could not understand how a world could be in a war, with itself? He exclaimed that the world was each and every one of the townspeople. He told them that any peace the community would experience would happen when everyone felt their own inner peace. They had to forget all disparities for it did not matter how each one spent their days, but that they did so for their own inner peace. In doing so, each one would listen to their own feelings, their own love, their own purpose. And as they would do this, they each would notice that their contribution to themselves was also a contribution to the whole community. They then were self-governed, no need of a dictatorial mayor and his council. The people listened intently as Butch spoke, for somehow they knew that he was speaking truth. With this newfound way of expression, the townspeople disbanded and quietly went to their homes feeling the love expressed in Butch's story. As this love became One within them, they, indeed, started to think differently. They each did what they loved. Excitement grew as each shared their stories anxious to relate their experiences.

This story, my friends, is your own story.

Note: The meaning of the name "Butch" is "manly" and "illustrious" (distinguished or esteemed among men; renowned; accomplished; worthy of recognition; commanding respect; eminent of actions).

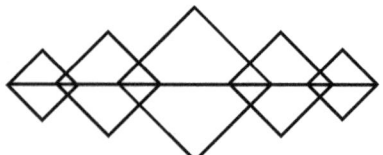

Q – Please explain more about the title of this writing.
A – The man, Butch, told truths and the townspeople began to understand his message because of the life Butch lived and how he easily survived and even thrived living his simple life. The tempest is the townspeople's attitudes with the discrepancies being displayed and spat upon by others, each one not understanding one another, and not holding their own responsibility for their very own lives, blaming others for their situations. The witch is the common denominator that brought the townspeople together to work out their differences. And that means the land that was toiled for the growth of crops and livestock. The witch is the celebration of the land or the knowing the importance of the land. It is the living nature of this reality.

Q – A witch, according to the dictionary, is a woman who professes or is supposed to practice magic; a sorceress. How does this meaning fit in with the living nature of this reality?
A – It is in this magic, so to speak, that the land is used for the growing of food stuffs. It is the magic of creation, the growing of foods from seed. Of course, the magic is only perceived as such for it certainly is not magic. It is the wave forms of the consciousness of the plant (and animal) kingdom making their way into the soils or earth consciousness. And that consciousness intertwines with the thoughts of the human, or in this instance, the thoughts of the townspeople. All is connected and all is ever so beautiful!

Q – In the beginning of this story, it says that a man decided to start an experiment trying to understand people and their interactions. This story is then his observations?
A – That man is also each one of you. Each of you contemplates your existence. So this is also your experiment, observing one another and yourself as you live in this world.

March 25, 2009

Sodium

We come to you today to discuss a very important mineral that is abundant in your Earth. This mineral you call sodium is a derivative of the metal like substance aluminum. Without this substance, your species could not survive as it is an important ingredient in the cells of the human body as well as all other animals and your plant kingdom. What you perceive yourself to be in this physical is perhaps a change in the antithesis of matter over matter. Matter is substance created in the physical by the thought forms of the human in relation to the overall thought forms of the soul encompassing all of the created forces you call Creator or God. In your Book 1 of Mystery of the Universes, you have discovered that you the human are part of a very large creator force and that you are the creators of your very own realities brought together on this Earthen plan of 3rd – 4th density or dimension. Each one of you has transcended the old thought forms that severely limited you in your acknowledgement of the creator forces within the body. You now know that you have come very far on this path you are calling ascension, and, indeed, you are. You are opening up your eyes and ears to understand what lives within your hearts. It is a masterful process.

Our discussion today centers around the body human and the created mineral, sodium. To live on this Earth Mother, your bodies need various amounts of minerals to hold your frequency to stay in the physical. And you want to stay in the physical so you can experience life in this limited dimension. The human body contains mostly water, up to 85% in most bodies. For the body to maintain this fluid, it must have other minerals to help hold this fluid in the cells. Salt, a derivative of sodium, is one of the substances that greatly enhances your well being. Its make-up of finely tuned crystals block the fast transference of water through the pores of your outer layer you call skin. It holds the composition of the water crystals within your cells. This process enables the human to be part of the Earth yet the water is that conductor of energy giving the life force the ability to move in this physical plane and connect to other planes of existence. As the human evolves within their consciousness, will you be able to more fully understand this process. This process then serves you with your body here and connects with your other bodies in other planes of your existence. What may seem as a miracle of life is just one of the processes most are not yet aware of. Be prepared to tune into the new paradigm of suppressed knowledge. Many of you are on the edge of understanding your earth physical body in relation to your other bodies.

The mineral, sodium, was created to be a part of this physical process. It enhances the molecular substrate within your body solid or what appears to you as solid. It actually is an element that conducts the forces within the blood and into the cells with its power to activate the chromosomes (in your DNA) to perform the protective barriers of the life flow. It helps keep the blood alive so to speak. It is a conductive apparatus with its structure of geometric form. Yes, it breaks down or is soluble in water, yet it maintains its form. You know this form as trapezoid. Under microscopic conditions, one is able to detect this shape. This shape is what holds its parameters in the locking in of cellular structure. Just know that in the patterning of the many minerals and elements, you will find that this is what causes the body human to withstand quick deterioration of the physical.

We are some of your planetary keepers (you have many). We bring you this knowledge for you to better understand the complex mechanisms that are a part of your human body. Treat your bodies with respect for they are to serve you, the part of your soul that has chosen to co-exist on this beautiful planet.

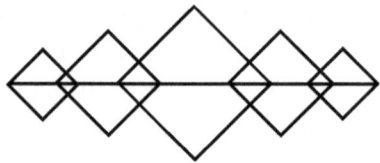

Q – According to the online encyclopedia under "sodium," nothing is said about sodium being a derivative of aluminum. Sodium, an alkali metal, looks very much like aluminum in a pure state. There are compounds or alloys of aluminum and sodium. Please explain.

A – There are refreshers on this matter, as this matter is changeable according to the number of electrons present in the process of elemental change. The properties of aluminum, found not as a pure substance in your organic as well as inorganic materials, are a malleable type metal substance. It can carry frequencies with ease in this pure state. However when coupled with sodium, you have different compounds, each having many uses.

Q – Are you saying that sodium is not a derivative of aluminum, as it says in this writing?

A – Sodium is its own element as is aluminum. This writing says that "sodium is a derivative of the metal like substance aluminum." Aluminum is a metal. Sodium aluminum silicate is a compound found most often in your earth. This is the substance this writing is speaking of.

April 12, 2009

The Turn of the Century into Biorhythms of Possibilities

You all understand that you are the ones who have come to this place called Earth to test the waters of possibilities while housed in the human form. All of you have lived other lives, many on this Earth at another time and many places on this globe. You also have lived and are living as other bodies on other planetary systems, some of these planetary systems you call home. Home can be anywhere anytime but a deeper meaning to being Home is living in all your worlds consciously, one life conscious of another life. You each have built your very own matrix that you are able to traverse at will. As third dimensional human beings, you had put on blinders so you are not able to see those inter-dimensional pathways. But as your Earth has entered into a new era, a new place within the cosmos, the blinders are coming off. Many of you can now see glimpses of some of your other lives, your brothers and sisters in other realms. As you find yourselves seeing into these "other worlds", you may become confused. Many of you do not feel that you are totally "here" or totally "there". Perhaps because each of you are sensing your multi-dimensionality. You are really right "here" which means you are also right "there". As you move into the rhythms of the higher dimensions, you will understand your capabilities.

Your Earth's turning on her axis gives you day and night, light and dark. In your night skies, you can see the millions of stars that shine and light up your dark heavens. Envision yourself as one of those stars shining your light with the other stars doing the same thing. Yet each of you have your "place" in those skies. You each have your own abilities, you are separate but when combined with the other stars, you can see a pattern. And that is the pattern of creation. It is the spiral of evolution, moving, morphing, creating, all within the same system.

Each of you are like each star that you see. You are evolving, moving, morphing, creating, all within the same system. You all chose this system to evolve not only yourself on this earth plane, but all of your selves, past, present, and future lives. You each have created this plan of being in this human form. You planned on being on this physical third-dimensional Earth. You planned on residing in the human form while at the same moment residing in your myriad other forms all simultaneously. Yet you chose your body that you live in, one created by you for you with the assistance of your family, your mother and father as you call them. So now what is happening to this body that you chose to live in inside this timeline you all developed? You have decided that this moment, you will take your creations (experiences) and share them with your other selves so that the big self, the god that you are (Higher Self) can determine what life is. What does it mean to breathe, to think, to love, to feel? This creation called the human has been a most wondrous adventure. And your adventures shall live on. You are taking it to new ways of being, while maintaining the physical form. You are melding it into the other aspects of the total you. And you are doing this with the total complex of matrices and lowered them onto the blue-green body of Gaia. Gaia, too, is merging with her other selves. She is moving, shaking, and aligning with her Higher Self.

As you and this wonderful Earth moved through the timeline of the new millennium, you have crossed into a new area of creatorship. Your brothers and sisters of the stars have come to assist in this process. Your other selves are all participating! This was arranged by you, creators combined. And now is the time of the great balance.

You have learned that you are energy, always in motion with the thoughts of your being. You are energy waves and particles always conversing with one another. You have developed these matrices to build this incredible cage of biology yet you are not contained by this biology. Now the cages are open for your biology to morph, travel, create in a whole other way of being. Note the changes that are happening within your bodies. You are re-connecting with the energy waves and particles of the higher dimensional you. And you are doing this along with the new birth within Gaia. She is moving with growing light within her belly. She is receiving "new" light (it really isn't new) as she manifests her new capabilities within her own matrix coupled with all of humanity. You are over the new horizon but most of you cannot yet see. See the light as it brightens on your horizon. See your own light as you look within your mirrors. It is physical, it is nonphysical, it is God shining through All. Your sun still shines brightly in your skies so you can see the light. You work with her (sun) and your connections bring you this wonderful feat of living in the physical world of form. Rise up, dear ones, in your knowingness that all is changing and changing because of your contributions of just being your god-self.

The Earth is changing into this being that shall accommodate your desired changes. It is only done in love for love of itself. Her light shall manifest through her skin. She is shaking and the land masses are moving. This is not to alarm humanity, but know that your wishes and dreams of a grand new world is upon you. Start living in harmony within your own matrix and you shall see this world change in the blink of an eye, the eye of creation. You have that power and now is the time for you to use that awesome power. Know in the deepest part of your being, that you are here at this auspicious time to be the movers and the shakers and the lovers. The Earth's skin is changing along with your very own bodily DNA. It is through the matrical connections that this is done.

See the light of the world come forth in your visions. Together you are making it happen. We salute you in all of your endeavors. We are here to assist. We are your brothers and sisters, the stars within the larger matrix of All That Is. Your thoughts merge with this matrix as it radiates out through the Holy Heart of Creator also known as The Great Central Sun. Your thoughts are your prayers. Let them be aligned with the divineness that you are.

Salute, Salute, Salute

We are the Grand Marchers who have come forth to share with you.

See "Mystery of the Universes", Book 25, Book of Entrapment. The Grand Marchers are also known as the Galeceans from Andromeda.

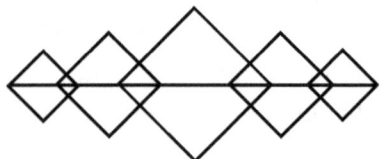

Q – What are the matrical connections?
A – What is being referred here as matrical is the divine lineage that each of you are linked to.

> Per the dictionary, matrical is an adjective meaning: of or relating to a matrix

April 13, 2009

As I have contemplated the above writing, information and visions received awhile ago came to mind, and I feel that this is the place to share this information. Around September 2007 my attention was drawn to the Earth's crystal core. I noticed that the crystal, also known as Earth's inner sun, started glowing brighter and brighter. After watching the History Channel on glaciers, and the quick melting of these glaciers at the poles, I went into an altered state of consciousness and saw red light circle the north and south poles, particularly the north pole. The circle was not solid and it glowed. I noted that the ends of the Earth were being sucked in with the equator expanding, the Earth changing its shape. On September 30, 2007, I received the following message:

Many changes, many changes. What you are seeing is your Earth reshaping herself. Indeed her center is expanding with her "ends" being drawn in. To accomplish this, her ice caps are melting. Initially your coast lines will flood as prophesized. Her center, the crystal core of her interior, is rising up and out. Her light within (the crystal core) is expanding to meet the demands of her interface with the Interglobal Society of Planetary Awareness. To this end, she is moving to her rightful place within this galaxy. She, Lady Gaia, is fully aware of her status as she expands herself into worlds whose planetary assignments, if your will, represent creation coming full circle in the auspices of the light of the Grand Creator. She is becoming a beacon of planetary service of physical creation.

You who live on her surface shall soon know of these changes. Your scientists and cosmologists and climatologists are starting to recognize the change of the lands under the ice. Now they recognize these changes as a result of the ice melting but this is not so.

What about the Inner Earth people?

They are adapting with this more powerful light emanating from this Great Sun within Earth's core. However they know that they will not be able to remain in Earth's interior much longer. They will slowly adjust their bodies to acclimate to Earth's outer service. Many of them will leave the Earth and make their living among the many starships encircling your Earth.

Be not alarmed as all of this is a part of Earth's evolution as well as you own. Be aware of your own personal changes. Love this beautiful Earth as she births her new self.

Then the crystal light within the center of the earth started splitting with the northern light spinning counter clockwise, and the southern light spinning clockwise much like a merkaba. On November 14, 2007, the two crystal lights spun faster and faster and "grew" apart until finally the light exploded through the poles, leaving a small red ruby light glowing in the center of Earth's core. Two other people who were watching this with me saw a pink light and rainbow light.

This inner Earth change also connects with another vision inside The Great Pyramid of Giza I have been having over the years. On January 1, 2008, I wrote the following:

Upon reading a book Journey to the Mystical Past *by Zecharia Sitchin, I came across information on a "secret" chamber not far from the Queen's Chamber in The Great Pyramid. I believe this to be the same chamber that holds the large crystal (dark blue) and another chamber (above this blue crystal chamber) with a rotating diamond (oval-shaped and somewhat flat on two sides).*

A few years ago in a vision I saw this dark blue lighted crystal change to a more turquoise color by the focus of four masters, each one standing on each side of the crystal. A couple years later, I noticed the oval diamond spinning clockwise, suspended above a square stone block. September 1, 2004, I noticed the large crystal also started to rapidly spin clockwise and even change to a gold light, back to blue/aqua- turquoise, to gold, etc. I was told that the spinning had to do with the sun and planetary movements. With the (recent) inner Earth major changes, I again looked at the pyramid's crystal and diamond. The chamber was almost dark with a faint bluish light emanating from the crystal's core. I also see the diamond lying on its side on the stone block. There was an intense connection of the pyramid's crystal and diamond to Earth's core. I asked Sananda (an ascended master with whom I communicate, also known as Jesus in one of his incarnations) about the inactivity of the crystal and diamond and was told they will be no longer needed. There is a dying out of the outer energy as it (the bright light) exploded within the Earth.

Per Sananda: "The moment of salvation of mankind is at hand. The miracles of yesteryear are the new images of the new world. Welcome aboard this New Earth."

I feel that this explosion of light is emanating from our Earth and this writing is saying to pay attention to this light from Earth and ourselves.

April 14, 2009

An Age of Understanding

You are now reaching an age of understanding with more depth into thoughts that originate from yourselves. You can sense the flow of energy as it penetrates your own body and flows out to touch others. You can see the changes within yourselves as well as within others. This is such a grand experience that you all came to be within this time and space of expanded awareness. Oh Creator Gods, you are on the brink of the next world ready to enjoy the fruits of your labors, those fruits of high expectations into the unknown worlds of form. You have reached your destination just in time to start plotting a new destination. You are always moving in the energy of the formless into the form. Such an incredible journey have you embarked on. Now is the moment that you each have been waiting for. It is now that you find your deliverer. It is now that you are ready to experience yourselves in greater fullness. It is done and it continues. It is that life form that you see yourself as. It is you in the energy form that you helped create. Your guides (also known as angels) have been with you all along because they are a part of you. They relish within themselves the related aspects of being in the human form to enjoy the many wants and desires of the soul to participate in the grandness of just being the great magnificent creations of the new world.

So now you begin. The journey is in front of you. The journey can also be behind you, along side of you or wherever you want it to be. It is a part of your expression. There is not one person on your earthen plane of existence that is not going through this change with you. It is their participation that makes this wonderful advancement in the state of being for humankind. You all have been to that space and time where you have known who you really are. You were given a set of blinders in the form of genetic manipulation. You allowed that to happen so you could finish your game of understanding the true force that you really are. Now that project is coming to a finish. No more hanky panky (human words!). Just the true divine taking its place of prominence in your vernacular.

Dear human, know that what you have accomplished is nothing short of truly magical. You may have heard that term before, magical. The trials and tribulations that you have experienced in your many lives have been very challenging. You even have taken some of those personal challenges from lifetime into another lifetime. Some of those challenges became a part of your own energy makeup within your body cells. And now those challenges are being shaken from you. You the god that you are, are allowing this program to take place. Surrender into that knowing. Do not let the old thought forms hinder your progress. In just a few of your years have you made the monumental task of releasing the old thought forms so the new energies of creatorship take their positions. Know within your heart that you are the One that you call God. You all are the One you call God. A new name is upon you and that name shall be Crea, the thought of Holy Creation. It is so because you have made it so.

April 15, 2009

The Time of Acceleration

The time of acceleration of the energies from the godhead is upon this auspicious earth. The turning of the lever that pulls the interference of divine energies into this area you call the system of Ra, is the receipt of information from the developers of the body human. Those reading this writing, know that the initial information on the seeding of the earth is written and explained in the first book (Mystery of the Universes) from this channel. We suggest you read those pages that tell of the many star systems that had their hand in the creation of the current human form. It now has been decided that the human is to go to levels not obtained in previous incarnations. The beautiful human is at the precipice of exceeding the original intent held for this form. The intertwining of the higher bodies into the lower thought forms has caused this massive shift that will be detailed into the new form. It is something beautiful and "miraculous" even within Creator, anything is possible. So time has changed, a new day has dawned, and everyone in the many galaxies wants to be involved in the process.

It is not yet known how the new system will manifest. Just know that you the human who are reading these words will be a part of total ecstasy living in the very heart of the love of

Creator. Yes, the new name is Crea, should this "event" even have a name. Until the divine right or the energy of salvation, the higher light (consciousness) being an integral part of the earth and the human form, is fully in place, then no system of life will have any control over any thought form that exists on the Earth. All life forms of the 5th dimension and above will be able to communicate with earth and her inhabitants, but are to leave all governments to those who are physically incarnate. There will be much sharing of ideas and technologies among the various on and off planet civilizations. The ones that are known as the Elohim will be closely involved in this endeavor. The Archangels will be the protectors of this process. Know, dear human, that you are a willing participant in this whole evolution. You came into your current body to be a part of this process. Know that all will be well and that you will feel much closer to "God" as you merge telepathically with your Higher Selves (the God that You are).

The Earth Mother is ready and is forming her body to accommodate this change. She is removing her old worn out cloak ready for the new creation to be her and you.

In sincere gratitude, we are the angels that surround each one of you. We love you dearly, always have and always will. Peace is eternal.

Q – The name, Crea, was first announced in the previous writing "An Age of Understanding." This writing also mentions Crea as an event, the movement into the 5th dimension. Is there more to this name that we should understand?

A – Yes, Crea is a shortened name for this transition. Create means to bring into being. And that is exactly what you are doing. Crea has a feminine sound although it includes both the masculine and the feminine as one unit. New humanity is and will be referred to as Crea.

April 20, 2009

The Watch

Some time ago, it was said that the Earth would be a magnet unto itself. That the world of On was to become a star that will shine brightly in the skies of the cosmos. It also said that many worlds would be changing at the same moment the Earth made her motion that the time was ready. As the Earth contemplated the arrangement set up by her with the others who would also be making profound changes, she decided that she would be the forerunner of a new technique. This technique is to balance the outcome, providing new ways of life in the great system Creator has provided. With the blessing of the other stars, with whom the Earth has made her decisions, has brought this sector of the universes, 3rd to 5th dimensions, into an understanding of the web all involved have provided. This plan, so devised by the heart of this planet Earth, became as the beacon to provide a sanctuary or place for Creator's creations to manifest new ways of being. These new ways shall be the forerunners of new civilizations that will manifest on other worlds in other galaxies.

What now has transpired is the reluctance of those who populate the outer areas of the planet Earth to live up to the terms in their agreements they made on the soul level of creation. With a nudge, the souls or higher selves are making their communications known to their unconscious lower bodies to move into higher conscious bodies. And this process has been quite a story for the whole of physically manifested beings. What is happening is that the bodies of physical life are maintaining their lower physical forms yet embodying higher forms of consciousness in which new types of manifestations shall unfold into a new galaxy. This new galaxy shall be a portion of the existing galaxies yet be a wavelength different, so the new creations are not hindered by the waves of the old thought forms of control. With the body of the Christed way of upper 5th dimension as a starting point, the human who resides on the surface of Earth and her sister planets will sublimate themselves into the new system. They will be known as the Star People of On.

Creator is forever expanding into new ways of being, into new universes. It is the inbreath and the outbreath, for they are essentially one and the same. They are creation within the light forces ever moving, expanding, contracting, expanding, contracting, yet within the wholeness of Being, seeking new ways of Being Creator. With the inclusion of the body human with the reassurance of their higher selves/bodies, has made this new creation or new way of life such a magnificent achievement of life everlasting. Those thought forms of these humans and their other selves have adjusted all creation in the new ways of Being.

Q - In the first paragraph, it is written that the Earth contemplated this great change as an arrangement she set up along with others and she would be the forerunner of a new technique. Who are these "others" and what is meant by "this technique is to balance the outcome?"

A – The others referred to here are the other worlds or planets, some in this solar system, and other planets in other solar systems, especially those planets or planetary systems that are working with you and Earth (Lady Gaia) on this transition. These were alluded to in the writing "The Time of Acceleration" which says that this information can be found in the first book *Mystery of the Universes*.

The word "technique" is used because the Earth is totally involved along with all humanity in this process. Duality, as you know, is coming to an end as you have known it. You will not be experiencing as much duality as you have previously experienced or are continuing to experience as the Earth and humanity bring the higher frequencies into their being. The outcome of this process or transition will give all a more balanced life negating the lower thought forms that will dissipate as you enter into the higher frequencies.

Q – This writing also says that humans on Earth and her sister planets who become part of this new system will be known as the Star People of On. In the writing "The Time of Acceleration," humanity will be called Crea. Are these just two different names for the new human?

A – Ah, you are correct in noticing the two names. The name Crea means the thought of Holy Creation, you creating, a process and a name. The world of On is your world or planet Earth. Therefore the name "Star People of On" is a group name including those called Crea.

May 1, 2009

Phase 1 into Phase 2

This seemingly huge transition that is happening in every sector of this universe merging into other universes has become one of the most astounding creations that Creator has ever known. This new definition of life shall be a precursor to new ways of living and manifesting new creations. The dawn or beginning of the transition started hundreds of earth years ago when it was decided that a new avenue or web of creation be put into place to help stabilize the new thought forms of creation. Next, the new web is also called a new dimension within a dimension, a new time line. What is occurring at this moment called time in the 21st century of recorded life, is the need for quantum physics to be turned on its head with a different set of physics to come into manifestation. In order for this to happen, the vibrational calibrations are changing into a whole new set of harmonics. All stations shall take their places in order for this new manifestation of life to occur. Take not what you have known, and be prepared to dream another dream. This new dream shall be the 2nd phase of this change. Phase 1 is now almost complete.

Those of us in the realms called angelic are ready with you to finish this plan. We are at our stations tuned into existing harmonics. With the release of Phase 1, we are ready to combine our efforts with you, the humans on earth, ascended masters, and accompanying star systems. We are ready to resume our place within the new constellations of new thoughts originating through humans with our assistance. We read the present and can see the future with its many possibilities, yet we cannot assume any of these possibilities coming into manifestation. The patterns we see occurring coupled with the change in harmonics (light and sound) makes for a transition of unprecedented thought forms. Indeed, a whole new horizon is rising with the new suns/sons in tune with the dreams of the All, everywhere in the universe now seen and felt on a multitude of dimensional levels. This stage of Phase 1, almost complete, will collapse and Phase 2 will rise from the ashes of old. The ashes will disappear as the newness of being begins. A completion, a beginning, and a newness, the excitement builds as the wheels within wheels are turning. It is time, or to be more accurate, it is the building of this new harmonic level of a new understanding taking shape. Humanity, you are the builders of this new tomorrow. You have taken your internal eyes into the gap to build, once again yet different, a paradise of unequaled elegance in the name of life, the living experience of the holy thought forms of each of you within All That Is. For this, we are most grateful and excited as we step into our positions to be the shoulders and strength for each of you to build upon. We are to assist you in any way we are directed within the holy state of Love.

We want to add that we are the harbingers of new ways of life but are not able to accomplish this without the input of the many thought forms coming from these other realms, specifically the humans. Because of humanity in their effort to shut down their knowingness of their connection to All That Is and then emerge from this sleep, has shown that life, indeed, will continue unabated through the use of this tool, the human form. Even through the many genetic changes, has the human not only survived but evolved through this sleep pattern which is now almost over. The awakening with the veils parted and then done away with will enable the human to fully connect to their own god-self so this 2nd phase will commence. Those of you humans, now know that this part of you is truly a miracle. You courageously came into the human form to experience the various intricacies of this creation. Many of you have come into so many forms, some of these forms where your divine knowledge was totally held from you, and other forms where you were very aware of your abilities. Evolution, devolution, and evolution, quite a process to be a part of.

In gratitude, we are the angels of love, always and forever more. It is said, it is done, and so it is.

May 11, 2009

The Solar Cross

Ages ago men came to this world to write their own story. Their ideas were not common to other world civilizations, so they came to this earth to share their interests in opening up communications with other worlds. They brought with them the power to communicate inter-dimensionally through the use of their own telepathic powers. They have the capabilities to audibly tie in to the other dimensions by creating a signal that is much like your own radio signals, yet have the ability to interconnect the webs that connect all life force. Intuitive communication will become the norm in the near future here on the earth plane, but it will develop into pockets or wave interference that transmit the waves through the use of the color wave cycles. This will enable the human to communicate with their brethren on other planets and ships that surround the earth. This technology has been used on the earth before this time known as the Great Millennium of change. However, through the great interference of some of the beings who came here to earth for their own agenda and which were not for the highest good of all, this technology came to an end. The lower dimensional frequencies were not a high enough vibration for this technology to work. Through the current changes, this technology will once again be commonplace.

Man will find remnants of this technology as they sift through some of the ancient ruins, cities built on cities built on cities. Also some of this technology will be found on your ocean floors as there will be much shifting of the sands. There are those men and women who will remember this technology as these items will be found. They will remember how it works and what to do to bring back this information.

Worlds upon worlds will open for man to see that, indeed, there are many civilizations beyond their own. They will become adept at finding information of their ancestry, personal as well as this earth's. Earth will also be known as the alive planet that she is. She will become more verbal as she shifts her sands, and her waters move to and fro. There shall be no question to her motive as she demands respect from all surface dwellers and those that reside on her interior.

It is still up to humankind to finish making their own internal changes as they move into their higher dimensional bodies. The makings that will occur will be so significant that man will not go back to the old forms of manifestation. No longer will man tolerate the old thought forms of limitation through their use of unbalance. Greatness and wonder of the magnificent life force that each one of us is a part of shall not be denied. The "radios" of tomorrow shall be an incredible tool for man to know himself as his own creator. The human cry has been heard, received through the banality of time/space. The Solar Cross is the tool that is the transmitter. It not only is a symbol of balance, but an inter-dimensional tool used to transmit voice and matter through its multiplex of frequencies.

We share with you, humankind, and those beings on other worlds who hold interest and sharing in the new worlds that are rising. Each of you, do not underestimate your capabilities. You are as the one you call the Risen Christ. Each of you is rising in your own power to know and understand the creative process. New worlds are opening on to you. The tools are for you to use and share. You are so loved.

When I was doing a search on the web for a drawing of the Solar Cross, I found similar designs to my vision below. Most drawings and photos I found of the basic ancient solar cross was a circle with the north/south and east/west axis contained within the circle. Upon seeing the cross below in my vision, I thought that it looked a lot like an old microphone.

Q – Please further explain a color wave cycle, a transmitter for the waves to enable intuitive communication. See paragraph one.
A – Each color of your spectrum has its own wavelength. In your visual spectrum, red has the longest wavelength with violet the shortest. The wave turns on itself and it is at this point the color waves morph into white light, then spread out again. This white light, a combination of the spectrum, interacts with the frequencies within your electromagnetic biological body, particularly the pineal gland, giving the human this capability of intuitive communication. Your pineal gland acts as a dissector in this instance. Your pineal gland, which, by the way, is changing as you take in the higher frequencies of light and sound, has the ability to be a recorder of information and dispersing this information to other parts of your brain. Therefore this gives one the ability to see and hear from other dimensional sources and within your dimension.

January 19, 2007

A Tour of the Village Amanhi

This book deals with a civilization that resided here on this earth thousands of years ago. They came to study the hologram that was forming by the thoughts of the ones who wanted to experience various densities of the physical yet remain open to Creator Source. These people participated in the development of the earth yet they did not fully adjust to the frequencies that were in place and were still forming. Herein is their story of their town and survival until they deemed it necessary to move from this earth. Their remains can be found in the deep Sea of Galilee. Most of the artifacts have disappeared through corrosion, however, parts of the artifacts can be found in the sifting sands.

February 18, 2007

A tour of our village is unique in that there are levels of attainment, levels of density, and levels of creatorship. We fit all of these together as we migrated to this region of the galaxy of Malkuth to study this earth and the bodies that resided on this earth. We came to understand ourselves in a whole different perspective as we changed the density of our beings.

We formed a kinmanship of elders who planned the community. They wrote a script of ways to live as a body even though we changed from form into the formless with our own will. We wanted to experience the various densities of energies moving through the spectrum of the seven rays. It became as a game for each of us to work out our plan to develop or create myriad forms with our thought patterns while inside our varying densities. We became as our own laboratories, creating and using ourselves in our own experiments. Our creations were interesting as we observed one another's way of creating.

What happened is that all of our creations did not mix well together so we broke up into groups or pods where each pod had free reign within itself. Our creations remained within our spectrums as we did not want to taint the civilizations that already existed on this earth and those civilizations that existed on other planets. We put ourselves in our own bubbles. With the various energies as we moved them into new or different forms caused our own bodies (both with form and without) to feel discord at our own manipulation of energetic forms. We created balance or we created discord.

The various pods were named according to the creations taking place within them. They were divided into the following groups:

Mitochondria[1]
Philosophical endeavors
Photosynthesis
Biological alterations
Chemical extrusions of biological bacteria
Sound transmissions within biology
Pyrotechnics
Hemispherical typecasts in zoological forms
Basic chemical compounds
Time used as a basis for understanding thought processes
Alchemical formations through basic thought

Each pod or division set out a list of goals in their experimentation's – basic density configurations with the input of creator source energy or energy of the greater mind. What we had learned was that we had total control over each of our projects as long as we participated in the higher evolutionary patterns of Holy Alcyone. Our creations evolved with use of the static mind. The static mind is another way of saying the energy of the void or nether. It is, it was, and it always shall be.

We have left the results of our experiments with those beings who populated most of the earth, those in the land of Mu. We have taken our findings into other realms of the cosmos to continue our technologies. We also continue with our experimentation of earth. We embody some of the greatest scientists that have documented their finds through the ages. Some of these men and women have incarnated in the isles of the Greek, the Egyptian, and the Atlantian. We understand time, and even though in the earth's timeline, these experiments were accomplished thousands of years prior to the great technological revolution of the new millennium. Thus, we have made an impact on humankind that reside on earth as well as those that reside in the center of the earth.

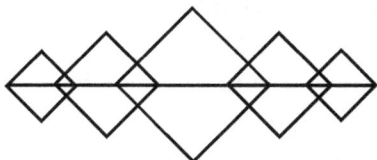

Q – This book does not go into the various groups and their endeavors. Is there additional information that will be forthcoming that explains some of their experiments?
A – There will not be any one book that follows this one. However, if one wants to tap into the knowledge of these people, they can by their asking. Much of the knowledge of the Amanhi people has been "forwarded" into this time through the work of the great scientists of ancient Greece, Egypt, and Atlantis.

When humankind further opens themselves to more interdimensional communication, then they will have direct access to the information that these beings have created and are creating. They, in essence, will be working together.

Q – Would you explain a little about each of the scientific processes of the groups?
A – Mitochondria[1] – cell division and arrangement of its parts.

Philosophical endeavors – the thought processes that affect cell growth.

Photosynthesis – the effect of light on all cell division in animal, plant, and mineral life.

Biological alterations – cloning, cell grafting

Chemical extrusions of biological bacteria – alchemical processes in the growth of bacteria

Sound transmissions within biology – understanding frequency within all matter and the manipulation of frequencies and their effect.

Pyrotechnics – the use of hot flame on the air and all matter

Hemispherical typecasts in zoological forms – the use of various hemispheres, i.e. chemical makeup, on various animal/biological life.

Basic chemical compounds – the mixture of myriad chemicals with simple thought patterns.

Time used as a basis for understanding thought processes – the use of time or linear thinking to accomplish scientific experiments. These beings were able to time travel.

Alchemical formations through basic thought – similar to the above philosophical endeavors but used additional research to understand the process of thought on the environment.

Q – We are learning to co-create or remember that we are co-creators. Is this just one of the processes that we can attune to?
A – All processes that have ever been and ever shall be are available to you now.
Wow!

---

1   Mitochondria per *The Living Webster Encyclopedic Dictionary of the English Language:* One of the minute, threadlike, granular bodies in the cytoplasm of the cell that is thought to function in phases of cellular metabolism.

May 18, 2009

The Condor and the Raven

The principal reality you have chosen to live in is now in the process of changing into a radically different set of chosen attributes. Each of you is now becoming your own new self, rising out of the old paradigm of limited understanding and living. You each have made the decision to end the parody, instead choosing to acknowledge your own beautiful selves as you have made them. There is absolutely nothing that can hold you back. Discard all the old thought forms of limitedness, because that is not the real you. Instead dream yourselves into the new reality that is forming from your holistic thought forms of pure manifestation of the spirit.

    Listen to every thought that comes to you. Some of these thoughts that pass through you, you can hold onto. Other thoughts discard immediately. All thoughts that enter your being are not necessarily your own. You are part of a huge matrix of the All, therefore the All has thoughts which is the combination of its seeming separated parts. You each have the ability to maneuver through all thought processes. It is such a wonderful dynamic that you have built for yourselves. You continue to build upon your own foundations of love made manifest into these wonderful beings of light that you truly are. The dream shall never cease, for God Creator Is and ever shall be.

Dream the dream. Live the dream. Wake up and you will know that you still are dreaming. It is the process of Creator Source. Know that prosperity is the forerunner of greatness. This prosperity is in all aspects of your being, especially on the earth plane of existence. Prosperity is your own acknowledgement that you remain in the dream.

Now the dream is changing and you all are feeling that this is so. You are seeing this with the huge changes going on in your world of form that you are dreaming. There really is no past and there really is no future. What is real is You. You have the capacity to move through this matrix of the All in you, power to move through the different colors and frequencies of the light. As you move your thoughts to the larger you, you have the capability to visit any part of yourselves in every moment, in every manifestation that have dreamed, or actually are dreaming. It is all happening now! This grand scheme you have invented to really know yourselves is known as the timelines that you have manifested and decided to live in. Until you realize that which you are, you will continue to build upon these timelines, making changes here and there. Here and there only exist within these parameters that you have built for yourselves.

When you are ready to fly, to see the whole picture you have built for yourself will you see yourselves as both the condor and the raven. The condor floats on the currents of the winds to become the wind. When it decides to know of itself as form, it will spot its prey, to become of its prey, then it moves on into the wind, with the wind, as the wind. The raven spots its prey, nourishes its body with its prey, then soars into the wind feeling the freedom of the air. These are two ways to manifest. Each of you is both.

June 15, 2009

The Round Table

In your myths and legends is the story of King Arthur and the Round Table. In this mythical tale, the Round Table serves King Arthur and his court. Even though there is much truth in this tale, told in another writing within this book (The Mystery of Avalon), we are going to focus on the meaning of The Round Table.

The Round Table signifies the truth of evolution. It congeals the notion that we, as humanity, are made up of transferable and transmutable energies. And in this process of alchemy do we know ourselves to be the fornicators of the new evolution of man into a more realized god. We set up this change, this radical change, that man and Earth are going through at this time. We have set up this change in the way we define our reality. We have set up this new dynamic of knowing ourselves in the Great I Am. We have done all of this, and we will continue on this mission of understanding ourselves and the many realities we have built. As we move forward through this thing we call time, we will realize that what we have set up, a new beginning, a new way of manifestation, has concurred with the frequencies of the force field, those thought forms which exited out from the central point of all physical existence.

In this process of redevelopment, we have fine-tuned the inert energies into active divine thought forms. We have made it possible through our own projections of peaceful intentions, those intentions coming from the source of our higher intelligence's. What mankind is now seeing and feeling in this third – fourth dimensional field of interaction is that those higher thought forms are making their way into the lower thought forms that have resonation to their higher selves. Humanity has been set up or made to resonate to those forms higher than their five senses can pick up within their physical body. However, their intuitive body, that 6th sense has been almost completely activated letting in the information that the higher selves have imprinted into the cells of the DNA.

Mankind is coming full circle meaning that they have broken free of the radical forms of existing in the physical without realizing their true identity. And now the masks of deception are being removed so man can look at himself (herself) in the mirror and know who he is looking at. Even this writer or scribe is having problems working with these words. These words are the thought forms of the collective consciousness. And this collective consciousness is that consciousness of the higher forms of intelligence of each and every one of you.

Know that it is you, each and every one of you, who are removing your masks to reveal your true identity. The dress-up party is almost over. Strip yourselves of these costumes and see yourselves naked. There is absolutely nothing to be ashamed of – that is part of the old paradigm that is slipping away.

The new identity is nothing new at all. It is you finally realizing what you had envisioned as being a part of humanity. You had set the stage and the old play is coming to an end. You, the actors and actresses are forming your new roles. What play do you wish to write and be a part of? Do you realize that you have written most of the play already? Now all you have to do is walk upon that new stage of understanding the cosmic you. This new play should be very interesting. It definitely will not be boring!

This fable of Avalon and The Round Table is a play that you envisioned and, indeed, it exists in another time and place, just a wisp away in another plane of existence. You can travel through the veils of the mists and see yourselves playing another role, if you so desire. It is your decision, always was and always is.

July 8, 2009

The Art of Transformation

There really is no art of transformation in the sense of the words. However, in order to transform, one must leave behind all ideas of control, the preconceived ways of transforming. Each one of you is continually transforming with new thoughts and new ideas coming through your dreams and imaginations. In order for your dreams and imaginations to manifest themselves, all you need to do is let go of how they will transpire in your life.

So really, why is this transformation called an art? Is it you, in all your splendor, reaching deep inside yourself to expose the wonderful inner world of divine essence to play upon the canvas of your external world, or what you see as your external world? As you have learned, there is no real external world. You have (or are learning) that everything that you perceive as out there, is only your projection of your inner reality. In a more simple explanation, the You that you are, a part or spark of Creator many of you call God, is a field of divine power ready for you to take these small particles, also called the Field of Possibilities, and trans-form them. This field is your playing field, and the many of you, including "others" that seem separate from you, are always trans-forming these particles.

Each one of you, that is each of you in your current life stream, are also many other life streams, perhaps in alternate planes of existence and realities. As each one of you become more conscious of your other selves, you will be able to tap into these alternate realities, making any transformation that you so desire manifest in this earth reality. It just is an exchange of particles. Your knowing that you are capable of such a feat will catapult you into new worlds of your choosing. Your technologies may be of assistance, but each of you has this innate ability. You are part of the system you call God, and within God, all is possible!

What is it you so desire? Let yourselves dream, because as you do this, you tap into these other realities. What an exciting adventure you gods have created! Indeed, isn't it interesting that you have all that you need right here and now? In order to become fully conscious of yourselves being your own creator, know you are love made manifest and nothing exists apart from this love. Any doubt you still hold will remove this conscious knowing. When you truly decide that you will live only in this love, dropping all thought of insecurities, fears and all lower thought forms, then you will be living in the New World. What are you waiting for?

God so loved the world that he gave his only begotten son of suns to be the passage of deliverance out of the chaos of not knowing the essence of reality. The thoughts left behind of your former teachers, including your beloved Jesus, have been written and passed through the ages, and thus have been manipulated into thoughts of subservience. Love thyself is you loving the god that you are. Go and play and create wisely. You are so dearly loved by those of us (and also parts of yourselves) who volunteered to be a part of this game of separation. The game has ended and it is in this now that your New World is manifesting through your thoughts emanating from your dream worlds.

We are the masters of old, but we exist in this now to be of assistance to the incredible beings you truly are. Namasté.

Jesus, as well as other teachers, taught these lessons of who we truly are or the essence of reality, or as stated above, he taught: "the passage of deliverance out of the chaos." However, his teachings were misunderstood, and these misinterpretations are what is still taught through most of our churches. The word "begotten" means "generated from," and all of us are generated from the One Creator. Each of us is a son, an aspect of our Higher Self referred here as "sun."

July 10, 2009

A Clear and Open Channel

Whenever I sit down to write another book (writing), I always say: "I am a clear and open channel, may it be for the highest good of myself and all that read it..." This title just came clearly to me, and I feel that this book will be most interesting for you, the reader, to know "how" this channeling, or interdimensional communication, works, and each of you have this ability. We shall see if this is so.

We shall see! What does this mean, we shall see? All of humankind has this wonderful ability, because each one of you is much more than this human body. In the first book of writings, "Mystery of the Universes," you have learned that you are a part of Source, can never be separate, as all exists within the One. So, of course, you have this ability! Each of you shall see, because it is a part of you. You are now tapping into the "more" of you and starting to see how creation works. Most of you reading this material are aware or know the Law of Attraction that has been explained through the many channels and will be proved in your scientific labs. You create your own reality, and in doing so, you create whatever is for you in every moment. Note that we did not say that you create whatever you want, even though that is what you are doing. It can be no other way!

To be a clear and open channel, align all of your thoughts with what is for your highest good. Sometimes you wonder why something pops up in your life, and then you wonder why it happened. It happened because you had decreed it so, the Law of Attraction. You may not think you did, but you did! There is no God out there that determines what is for your highest good unless that is what you ask for. You think that your thoughts are private, when in Reality, there is no such thing as private. Your thoughts move the life force into action. That is what this god that you are does always.

Remember the time when you were a small child and you thought, in your meekness, that life could give you whatever you want. Well, you were correct! However, in the communication with your family, you could not communicate to where they understood your motivation. So you did not receive what you wanted. Your thought was there, but the communication centers were not developed enough for your thought to be transferred to the person it was directed to. Now you can understand why children cry and carry on when their thoughts are misinterpreted or, in many cases, ignored. Such frustration! You may have noticed that this has carried on into and through your adult lives. It is through proper communication that this Law of Attraction works, and your way of communication is changing.

Memory serves you in many ways. It tells you where you have been, what you were doing, and how it felt in these processes. Now you are moving out of this old paradigm into a new understanding that will catapult you to new heights within your consciousness. What this means is that you will no longer tolerate the business of being in mental and physical constructs that limit you. You always have had free will, that diminutive process that says you are a mere human. Now you are finding out that you are so much greater than you ever imagined! Okay, now imagine anything, anytime with whoever bridges a dream or thought. You play in tandem with one another to fulfill those dreams and thoughts, that state of inner consciousness before you bring them into your physical reality.

In your explorations of this incoming reality, you will find that you are in total control, that god within each one of you. You each have your own string that attaches to what you call your solar plexus, for, indeed, it is as a gateway much like your physical sun within your solar system. What was once your feeling of "why has this happened to me?" into "I have created this so…". The new world awaits you. You are now getting glimpses of this reality. It is set and ready. All you need to do is accept the loving grace that is yours (and always has been yours) and take it into the new life forms that shall precipitate a whole new consciousness. Your memories of the old shall fade away, for this old life form is finished. For most of humankind, it shall not "return" into your lives, unless you want to play in that denser energy. It is up to you. So what do you choose?

Certain pulses of life will rain down upon you pulses come through the divine uniqueness of your Higher Self. The total You is in control and you are not controlled by any other force. Know within your heart that you have made this transmission into the most exciting adventure of all "time", or all creation. Fly high and enjoy the ride.

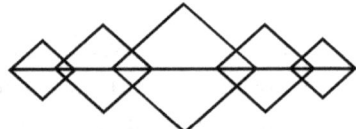

Q – Why is free will called a "diminutive process"?
A – Free will was instituted in this third dimension paradigm of limited understanding. What could you, as god, create? It is such a divine process, and humankind has done well to experience their perceived separation. Because of the perception, each human being felt lowly, not able to understand the god force in all reality, a diminished understanding.

July 27, 2009

Basic Understanding of Breath

The breath of life is in the hands of gods, your manifestation of your physical reality, that in which you perceive you are living. Each one of you has delivered into this reality that which you perceive life to be and how you want to be in this paradigm. Yet you manage to circumvent many activities that were in front of you and you pretended that they did not exist. Your reality made them non-present! As you have begun your ascension to a more realized understanding of how life works, you find that your body changes as well as everything around you. It is like you are seeing life for the first time in rose colored glasses. As you remove your spectacles, you will find that life in the world of third dimensionality has brought you to a new place of understanding. Your duality that has been experienced has given you a new perspective of living within the form. Now the tide is turning, and the duality is changing into a more cohesive frontier of living together in the physical. Not only will all life be perceived so much different in the new Golden Era, but the mere act of using the human body will transcend anything you ever have dreamed possible. This indeed is the new era, worlds coming together to migrate to a whole other existence. We do this together, knowing that we are not separate. Never have been and never will. The new reality will be so much easier to comprehend how and why we manifest the way we do.

The words that you use in your day to day activities will even change as your thought forms progress to the level of knowledge that you create everything you see, think, and feel to the extent of your making another existence out of the form you call your heart chakra. You breathe in the air, the composite of oxygen and nitrogen. It gives life to the body as the exchange of nutrients through your blood system, that crystallized system, feeds the biology. This system called breath also feeds the internal knowledge that you have within your very own genetic system. You have carried this system forth as you have reincarnated in the various bodies of form to build upon the understanding of knowledge brought here to this part of the universe, to be the diverse challenge of manifestation using the love quotient, the individualized parts of the Creator. You shall know all of what we tell you within your very own cells as they duplicate themselves to bring you to a higher understanding of what it means to be in the physical. The making of a new reality is forthcoming. It is here in the sense that all existence is here, you just tap into a very small part of it.

The dreams of yesteryear are now your reality. Those forms that have built this stage of life are now coming to a close so you can move on to build bigger mountains in the stream of thought. Now is the time to breath deeply in the parts of yourselves you forgot were even a part of you. Bring them forward so they can appear within your present reality. Know that all decisions are yours alone. You make them and all form shall follow. What a wondrous opportunity it is for you to know that you are a major player in the world of form.

We love you very deeply. We walk with you with every footstep that you take. We are family.

August 6, 2009

The Great Call

These times and these coming times called The Great Call is now, in this moment, a beckoning to all who consider themselves the finer aspects of God Creator. It is with our utmost gratitude that we share the following with you. We are the fine tuners so to speak. We work with the fine detailing within your system you call hu-man. We facilitate the changes going on with the Earth and all who reside on and in her. She sings her song of true glory of creation. She brings herself forth to show that she, Lady Gaia, can shake off all programs that are not in tune with her song. She can shake off all who try to inhibit her being, her energy, as she soars to the new cosmos of creation.

We welcome all who are here and are coming to this wonderful planet of Creator in the physical. We honor you who read these words because you know who you are. This time of the great separation is coming to a close. The Earth, our dear Lady Gaia, is saying that it is her time to move on to other forms of existence within this one kingdom of creation. She moves with the utmost splendor tuning into the finer frequencies of physical life many on Earth call the fifth dimension. Most of this information is not new to you but we say, it is. For you to embrace what is happening on this grand scale of cosmic delivery is an astonishing act of bravery and love to all that take part. So it is you, dear reader, that is coming forth out of your cocoon to be counted among the living force of manna. You are remembering, going into that still place within that says, yes, I Am. I Am the Kingdom, the Power, the Glory, Forever! I Am!

To declare that which you truly are is one giant leap into the new worlds of form. Leave behind all that got you to this place and time. Honor yourselves as you leave the safety of your cocoons. Be not afraid, for there is absolutely no fear to where you are going. You are not leaving anyone behind, because there will be no behind. Some of your thoughts and feelings will dissipate as if they never existed. Just know that you have made it, made it past the old feelings of despair. These feelings will never enter into you again for it is not possible.

The new world that you will inhabit will be a combination of societies that will blend themselves into a new matrix of belief, knowledge, and wisdom. This knowledge paired with the incoming frequencies of a new grand order is in place in what you now call the outer realms. However, those outer realms are being integrated within your very being. The Golden Age is here, you have made it so, but so many of you have yet to realize this grand order.

Your societies will blend themselves in new ways. The many corners of your Earth have housed many civilizations, some very advanced. These communities will again spring forth in your new world. They did not leave, but you see them not. Your new perceptions will show them as new, but know they have existed for many millennia.

They know that you are coming, and that you will live side by side, and will share with one another. What you will witness is such a grand opening into the "now" way of being, that you will quickly forget that you existed in any other way.

We tell you to be ready and willing for this great transformation. It is happening and you definitely are seeing the old crumble as many scurry to and fro wondering how they are going to live. Live they will if they so desire. The old is crumbling under your very feet and before your very eyes. Let it go. See the beauty that waits beyond. It is truly magnificent.

Just know that we are your brothers and sisters awaiting your return so we all can soar together into the new age. Understand the peace within you, it is there. Tap into that knowledge that is in your cells. You have carried this with you in all of your incarnations. It has been activated and will continue to be more fully activated as you rise in your consciousness. A new you is being formed. Many of you think you are ill for interesting manifestations are incurring within your biology. It is you transforming from a mere biological creature to one who knows their place within the stars. You are the crystal children, those who are now incarnating into the physical, as well as those of you who have been on this Earth for many years. Notice the change in your sensory perceptions. Notice the change in your emotional states. Notice the changes in your eating habits. Listen to that inner voice, it will tell you what it needs. The new world is here waiting for you to join her as you make your way into the new heavens.

June 17, 2007

The Focus of the Moon

There was a time when man worshipped the moon as the all-seeing and the all-knowing life force that penetrated the ground of the earth. It was decided that the moon was an instrument of poetic power that could raise the dead and manipulate the body human. When it became known that this was not the truth, the seers of that day set about a dance that took place during the waning of the moon, so that a new moon would follow. Some tribes today refer to this dance as "the tribal rebuke," now knowing that the moon effects their sleeping and awake patterns. The following information will give you a whole new perspective of your moon. This information applies to many other moons that circle other planets, yet not all moons have this capacity.

An arrangement was made during the storm of cosmic debris that a satellite would be made available to stabilize the earth in her orbit around the sun. Through much discussion by the ones of the realms of most high, the Elohim, it was agreed to position this satellite above the earth's surface just above her dense atmosphere. This satellite is made up of portions of the star Anochian that exploded leaving a small but dense center of crystallized iron. Yet through this body does the capacity to inhabit the senses come to play within this spectrum of the life force called human.

The welcoming of this fine jewel, this portion of the Anochian star, attracts the body magnificent of the star dust within the mere tunes of matter coalesced around the portal of the crystalline center. This gem, the earth's moon, is such a spectrum of divine energy assisting this beautiful earth orbit the large fiery ball of sol. However, this new form has properties that include more than assuming the role of progressiveness of movement. Within this great crystal are memories of a once great civilization that existed in the realm of form that served its intelligence the making of fine instruments of poetic powers. These fine powers include the delivery of harmonic resonance, thus the power to persuade the evolvement of humans in their manifestation of the mind. The sensory downloads that the mind receives are through this portal of light embracing the love of Creator in the breaking forth the instrument of the voice and the ears. Hence this tool that the human enjoys is for the more full experience of being in the form. What this power fulfills is the poetic justice that is received through the medium of the secular diminutive point within the glandular sequencing of light and sound. This is accomplished through the thyroid gland, that major gland within that controls these vocal tools and the ability to resonate with various frequencies.

Many people can actually hear the moon sing. These frequencies open the mind to receive information regarding a more pure form of being that resides within each one being. Each one's tune or vibration can be enhanced with the projecting of consciousness to the (moon's) center crystal. This helps clear the mind of any debris caused from misuse of the body or misplacement of thought forms.

There will come a time when the moon shall shift in her position and become one of the centers of stabilization of the new galaxy forming. As the planets in this solar system change their positions as they near the new center star in the Galopian system, also known as Sirius coupled with Orion, the moons will gravitate to their new positions. The human will be able to work with the frequencies of additional planets and moons. This will greatly enhance their abilities to manifest new light and sound, otherwise known as new creations.

This book is written within the crystals of your moon. You can access more information with your focussed intention to the moon's central core. You now have all of these abilities within you. Enjoy manifesting with even more clarity. You will feel as though you "have arrived", yet there is so much more for the human to realize within your evolved growth. Go with God and with god.

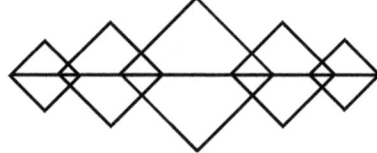

Q – In paragraph 2, this writing says that our "sensory downloads" of light and sound come through the crystal within the moon. Do all of our (human beings) sensory downloads of light and sound come through this portal?
A – Hummm, you just called your moon a portal. Do you understand why you call this a portal?

Q – Because the moon enhances our senses "through" the crystals? This writing also calls the moon a "portal of light."
A – Each of your body's contain crystals like that in your moon. It is essentially the same substance. All is connected, and the strength, so to speak, of the moon's crystals are immense and very obviously affects all life on your planet. So to answer your question regarding all of your body's sensory downloads come through the moon is no. However, because of the strength of the

moon's crystals, then the portal of which the moon is for these energies, indeed the moon is the major force that connects and activates the human for better reception of light and sound.

Q – Toward the end of this second paragraph, what is meant by "poetic justice received through the medium of the secular diminutive point with the glandular sequencing of light and sound?"
A – Poetic justice means that the rhythms of this energy gently flow as do words in a poem. The word "secular" means worldly or not bound by monastic vows or rules, therefore your earthly body living with free will. In order for you to perceive and experience light and sound, your body is made up with glands.

Q – I have "seen" geodesic domes, space ships, and people, human and what we term aliens, on the moon. Are they effecting the moon's center? Are they working with this energy or what?
A – They have no affect on the moon's frequencies. They do use her gravitational force that is part of her center crystal core, but it does not alter her frequencies.

Q – I have heard it said that the moon represents the unconscious mind and the feminine.
A – Yes, the moon does affect the unconscious mind, yet what is happening with the human race is the opening of the unconscious into the conscious. Therefore, the moon is actually a tool for the human mind, is it not? It is called feminine because it nurtures the mind (and body).

Q – In Mystery of the Universes, *Book 23, "Book of Tibet," it reads: "The time will come when the planets in this particular solar system will combine with those of the star gate system called Sirius." This book states the planets in this solar system will or are changing their positions as they near the new center star in the Galopian system, Sirius coupled with Orion. Please further explain.*

A – There is a passage in your book that reads that the star systems are all changing, not only this earth. Indeed there is movement of all the systems, some you cannot yet see from your earth due to the light years or the amount of time it takes for the light to show itself to the earth. Both the Sirius system and the Orion system are moving where they will maintain a closer proximity to one another during the next phase of your rotation around Alcyone.

Q – How close will the earth be to Sirius and Orion? Also when will this happen?
A – It is happening now. It is a process where there will be a warp in your space/time line that will move the earth without your even realizing that you are moving in such a fast pace. Your earth is so protected with her atmospheres, that there will not be a big glitch happen within her atmospheres. However there are weather anomalies now happening upon your earth and within your earth. These changes will continue. Your shore lines will expand in some areas and decrease in other areas. New mountains will form as others will flatten out. Many, many changes are going on and will increase in intensity. Man will survive and even thrive as man moves into a more realized light body. Those that stay in darkness or the more dense form will not be able to handle the changes and will just leave the planet, most probably through death of the body. They will have an opportunity to continue their lives on other planets of like density.

Once the earth is more stabilized in her new position, the skies will clear and you will see major changes in the locations of suns, planets, and moons. This whole process is quite remarkable. Are you ready?

Q - Have our astronomers noticed any major changes in our skies?

A – Many more of your astronomers have noticed some changes with the use of more powerful telescopes. With all of the information they are receiving through your Hubble telescope, they are seeing what they term miraculous events. So their science is changing to keep up with their findings. Physicists are working alongside your astronomers working to understand what they are witnessing. They are noting dramatic changes in our atmosphere, Earth's magnetosphere, Earth's gravity, and the movements such as the increase in earthquakes and volcanoes. They have a lot of data they haven't yet published because of their not wanting to alarm the populace. Some of these scientists know why these changes are happening. But many do not understand or want to understand the whole spiritual awakening that is now taking place.

Please note that when I first channeled this question in June 2007, I was told that the astronomers were not seeing any major changes. However, today in this year 2010, I was asked to change this to the above information.

Q – *Can you tell us more about the Anochian star?*
A – The Anochian star system has parted ways and have become parts of other star systems. Your moon in particular was one of the small planetoids that maintained its central core that was very magnetic, thus it attracted a lot of dust particles as it moved through the cosmos. It was brought here by means of tra-versing through time and space by the manipulation of the space/time warp, much like your infinity symbol, a twisted loop. It was heralded here by Lady Gaia herself with assistance from a fleet of ships you know as the Ashtar Command. They used their largest Mother ship with smaller ships following behind in the shape of a V, the moon being in the center behind the Mother ship. It looked much like your watching a flock of geese. The large instruments on the Mother ship acted as a large magnet that pulled on the core of the planetoid bringing

it into position near to where it now is.

I found this interesting information from NASA regarding Apollo 13's flight to the moon launched on April 11, 1970:

> At 7:21 p.m. Tuesday, the spacecraft swung behind the Moon, lost contact with Earth and passed 164 miles above the lunar surface. Haise and Swigert, who had never been so close and might never get closer, snapped photos like a couple of tourists. At 7:49 the spacecraft emerged on the other side and was again picked up by tracking stations.

This conversation took place:

SC--Houston, Aquarius.

CAPCOM--Aquarius, Houston.

SC--The view out there is fantastic... You can see where we're zooming off.

> Apollo 13 was headed homeward. Moments later the 15-ton spent third stage of the Saturn V launch vehicle crashed into the Moon, as planned.
>
> It occurred at 8:09 p.m. EST, April 14. The S-IVB struck the Moon with a force equivalent to 11 1/2 tons of TNT. It hit 85 miles west northwest of the site where the Apollo 12 astronauts had set up their seismometer. Scientists on Earth said, **"the Moon rang like a bell."** *(my emphasis)*
>
> Back in November 1969, the Apollo 12 astronauts had sent their Lunar Module crashing into the Moon following their return to the command craft after the lunar landing mission. That Lunar Module struck with a force of one ton of TNT. The shock waves built up to a peak in eight minutes and continued for nearly an hour.
>
> The seismic signals produced by the impact of s-IVB were 20 to 30 times greater and four times longer than those resulting from the LM crash. Peak intensity occurred in 7 minutes. The information from these two artificial moonquakes led to reconsideration of theories proposed about the lunar interior. Among puzzling features are the rapid build-up to the peak and the prolonged reverberations. Nothing comparable happens when objects strike Earth. One theory is that the signal is scattered and repropagated in very deep rubble. Another holds that the velocities of seismic waves from these impacts are comparable to measurements of velocities in crystalline rock. So the crystalline material which the astronauts found so abundant on the Moon's surface may extend very deep into the Moon.

August 7, 2009

The Face of Tomorrow

Tomorrow is today's thoughts materialized. It is in the moment that you exit your ability to move mountains. However, in each of your moments you create movement, and it is this movement that moves the mountains. More simply put, you live your dreams as you dance (movements) as a result of your thoughts. The movements which are now taking place upon this wonderful jewel that you live on and partner with, are combining with the knowledge of the stars that have combined themselves here on this plane of existence right here on this Earth. It is this dance, this movement that precipitates the changes that are occurring in your lives. Once you fully understand this co-creative process, you will know that, indeed, the eagle has landed. Your eagle represents the freedom of flight with a prowess to seek its prey. The eagle has the eye to see and interpret the events that unfold below the spread wings. It knows its position and the time for it to attack its prey. We liken this to you, dear humans, where you are ready to strike your prey. The prey is those ideas of peace coupled with the new thought patterns that are coming to the forefront within your beings. Your thoughts are being electrified, enhanced, for a clearer projection. The knowledge that you have held within is being vibrated to let loose into your consciousness of understanding.

As you exit your bodies in the time of great change, know

that again you will occupy a much grander form that is mutating at this very moment. It is these moments that interpret those thoughts that will release you from any bondage that you have set for yourselves in earlier earth years. The spectacle about to take place is ready to come or meld in your plane of existence. You will see the fiery lights as they sparkle over your heads. You will witness the destruction of the old earth that will return no more. The old earth will vanquish to allow the new earth be birthed from the interior of her body. She now gives birth and you are the mid-wives. Ever so gently catch the new vibrations in Earth's beingness. Perhaps catch is the incorrect word to use because each one of you is an integral part of this earth and because of this, you feel her pains as she releases the old to open for the new world to completely manifest itself in the realms of the most high.

As you view the situation that you now witness on this Earth plane, see the vulgarities as they are being shown to you. Man, have you learned that trickery and abuse no longer provides for you? No man can continue to ride the waves of deceit for soon there will be no waves to ride upon. You will witness a continuous outpouring of love made manifest within the very heart of each and every one of you. So what will this Earth look like? What we see coming forth is a brilliance of manifested rainbow light seething from every object, every human, and the Earth herself. The light shall shine brighter and brighter as humanity releases the garments of old. The brilliance of the colors will be so magnificent, it will capture the eyes of your many friends who do not sit upon the Earth, your space brothers and sisters. You will be interacting with these friends as they visit you in your homes and businesses. They, too, are a part of this transformation process. You will feel their wonderful vibrations and you will embrace them as family, for indeed, they are family.

You will witness a much grander form of being with your

strengths magnified, physical as well as mental. Technology will seem to vibrate from your inner core and your travel will be as easy to just think where you want to be, then you will instantly be there in your full garb of physicality. Foods will be plentiful and the menu will include vegetable, fruits, and nuts, along with your grains. The animals will no longer tolerate giving their lives as a food source. And the process of eating your animal parts will be as eating your fellow man. Your animals will serve you in ways you have not yet thought of, and you will see the changes in your animals starting now as they, too, are mutating.

Your atmospheres will also see changes in their colors that vibrate in their "shields." The sun will shimmer with more iridescent hues. In time the sun will fade and you will notice that the light of day comes from within the Earth and yourselves. You will be positioned in a different space within your solar system. In fact, the whole core of your solar system will change, your rotations will change. The term "solar system" will change to another name called a "light system." And this light system will be positioned in another arm of your Pleiadian system as it moves into the Anochian star system of Sirius.

Humankind, you have developed this form that you inhabit into a synchronized biology with your space brothers and sisters. Your abilities to move about the various planets will be much easier in your new forms. Your consciousness will seem as if it entered into your twilight zone. Brothers and sisters, watch with an inturned eye what is actually happening on this beautiful Earth. A most amazing feat is being accomplished. All worlds applaud you.

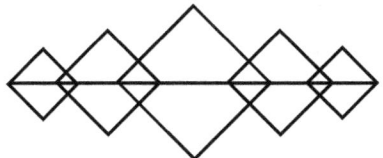

Q – The first sentence of the second paragraph, it is written "as we exit our bodies." Please expand on this concept of exiting our bodies.
A – In many of your writings within this book, you now know that your bodies are going through a lot of changes. Yes, you will exit your bodies through some of the more drastic repositioning within your structure. You will remain attached to your bodies, and removing yourselves (an actual out-of-body experience) from your physicality will allow for a much easier transitioning for most of you (humanity). This will happen in small increments of time allowing your bodies to absorb the higher frequencies with greater ease.

Q – In the writing "The Focus of the Moon," see Book 52 from this text, it says that our moon is made up of portions of the Anochian star which exploded. Please explain what is the Anochian star system of Sirius.
A – Your moon, indeed, is from the exploded star called Anochia. The Anochian star system of Sirius is also a remnant of this same system from which your moon came. The Anochian explosion produced many pieces and as these pieces whirled around a central core of strong magnetic energies, they became intertwined making a strong field pulling in more debris. Your Earth is being pulled in that direction.

I see a brightly shining group of matter, like a bright group of close planets/stars that looks much like a ball with many parts.

Q – In the same above referenced writing, "The Focus of the Moon," it is written that the planets in this solar system will change their position as they near the new center star in the Galopian system (Sirius coupled with Orion). Is this Anochian system part of the Galopian system?

A – Your current solar system is now and will continue to be part of the Pleiadian system. Pleiades is being "sucked" into this new system called Galopian.

Q - *The Earth is part of the Pleiades?*
A – When you take in all of the closer star clusters and view them from afar, you will see a much larger system with a central core, Alcyone at the center, with huge arms spiraling around it. Your solar system is located in one of these arms.

Q - *I see a galaxy that is becoming less "flat," more rounded. This new system, or clustered ball, is located toward the outside of this larger Galopian system.*
A - The gravitational fields in the whole of these systems are changing. So, yes, what you see as a ball, the Anochian system, is part of the Galopian system.

Q – *Currently the center of our galaxy revolves around Alcyone. Will Alcyone continue to be the center of this Galopian system?*
A – Yes. Please keep in mind that you as humans, in your co-creative processes, will be as the new gods on many of these new planets and planetary systems. In the woven tapestry of God Creator, this change adds another layer of realized experience in the whole of the plan. Remember, each one of you is an integral part.

October 23, 2009

The Pump

Now is the moment when all people shall come to be known as the winners of a very incredible project. This project has been talked about many, many times, even within these writings. This project you all volunteered to be a part of. This incredible project is known as The Great Experiment. What you may not know, but are learning, is that each one of you have put into this project your knowledge, your principles of life combined into a synthesis of awareness studded and confined in the form. This form is not only the physical body that you now occupy, but all of the other physical bodies you inhabited when experiencing life on this third dimensional experiential plane. Your memories of other Earth lives remain within your physicality, within the very chromosomes of your DNA connecting you to the Book of Records that each one of you are still writing. You also have remembrances of some very early Earth lifetimes where you lived in altered states of consciousness, able to commune with other life forms, on and off the Earth. Using the term "altered" is actually living within the true body, and you are remembering that you are able to do this without any hampering of the low density of energy that slowed all processes of life into a combined effort of forgetfulness. Once you break out of your cages each one of you has built, you will see a much grander life that is yours and always has been yours.

The possibilities are always available within the context of creation. You will absolutely remember that You are the Creators, that is, really, there is no out there out there. And you will position yourselves as the Grand Masters that accomplished this incredible project. This project has now accomplished what you all decided to accomplish, and that is to understand the nature of You in its many aspects even within the fields of an extremely low vibration.

You will now take this information, this life form of the physical and play with it some more. Indeed, that is what each one of you are doing – playing with and within your life forms. But now you are adding to the equation so to speak. What we mean by this, is that you are adding on to the experiences you wish to have by incorporating an increased understanding of your Higher Self, that energetic part of You that maintains its presence in the physical, yet in a whole other frequency form. You now know that all is energy, that what you call God is actually this energy transformed by the overall thought forms of your combined Higher Selves. It is One split many times.

You now have a saying "take this to a whole new level." You are taking your present physicality to a whole new level. In doing so, you are acknowledging you have succeeded on the 3rd dimensional plane of manifestation, and you are moving to a new time capsule (time and space) prepared by you for you.

The Earth is now splitting, not in the 3rd dimensional physical sense, yet it is physical. You know that many will remain in the 3rd dimension while most of you will ascend through the 4th into the 5th to the 7th dimensions. And you will do this using the basics of this physical body, yet your current physical bodies are being adjusted to accommodate higher energy frequencies. In the coming days, you shall notice these changes, and these changes cannot be mistaken for a major illness. One, you shall be totally aware of what is happening in and around you. You shall know what you experience is just you going through the changes as you begin to more easily communicate with the other parts of yourselves. There will be no fear accompanied with this process, as we have stated before, all fear will diminish upon this Earth. This is the Earth that is transforming itself along with you humans who have volunteered to be a part of the process of Earth. There is no other Earth that has been prepared, unless you call your current Earth one of "old," no longer able to retain the lower frequencies, and the now ascending Earth, the New Earth. This Earth is one and the same, yet has the same capabilities as the human to transform herself. There will be no lift off of humanity to "save" humanity from calamities or to transport to another planet, such has been reported. Each of you is your own savior. However, you do commune with "others" that are in different forms, living on other planets, planetoids, and ships, many of these stationed in other dimensional frequencies.

This writing is for you to understand that many processes are now taking place and you are witnessing these changes at an unprecedented rate. Know that you will open up to your many aspects and understand the processes that are unfolding. Your consciousness takes "trips" to other parts of Yourselves, leaving you in a spaced-out mind, because your mind and inner consciousness are more present in another time and/or space. Sometimes you do walk around in a zoned-out state, but return to be present in this presence. You will be leaving and returning, wondering where you were. Just know you will soon begin knowing where you are at all times, and in all frequencies. You will be able to handle You in all of your frequencies, yet have the capability to focus in one or two of these frequencies at any one time, yet you will understand that time is just a way for you to focus in the denser frequencies.

Realize the uniqueness of being human. Know that your life upon this Earth in this moment is your undertaking of the life force into the sacred archives of knowledge. This is your place, yet know that place is just a way to look at your creations. What you are witnessing is this Grand Plan taking form out of The Great Experiment, reaching new levels of understanding within the total matrix of Divine Creation. Watch your skies through your telescopes and the smallest particums that you can view through your microscopes. There is change happening everywhere. There is movement, there is momentum. Indeed, you have moved to new levels and are ever moving into extended states of consciousness.

Know that we are you in your other states. We speak at this time to tell you that we have come, come into the understanding that you have put forth in this matrix of divine celebration. We speak as outside of yourselves, but we are very much a part of each one of you reading these words. As we said earlier, there really is no outside. What appears as outside is your projections into this time capsule. You are like the projector and those you see are in your projections. An interesting way of looking at life. You have succeeded and are transcending the old plan. This new plan is now taking shape out of your projections into a new capsule, yet you have the means to move anywhere, anytime. The heart of any matter is your pump into new worlds of form.

On November 2, 2009, I channeled information for answers to conflicting channeled information by others, and some of this relates to this writing "The Pump." I do understand that other channeled information may be different than my own. You, the reader, use discernment in all you read and hear. There are many untruths being told for numerous reasons. I do personally question a lot of the information I have received in my channelings because a lot of it seems "far out." The following is one such "far out" information I asked about.

Q - I have just read (from another source of channeled information) that there is an imminent stasis period (a period of suspended animation for all life forms) and many humans will be teleported onto a space craft as the earth goes through a pole reversal. In one of the books I channeled "The Pump", dated October 23, 2009, it is written that there will be no lift-off of humanity to save humanity from calamities or to transport to another planet. What is happening here where we are receiving conflicting reports as to what is happening to Earth?

A - There are many concepts and channels "floating" around on your Earth plane regarding what is happening within this ascension process. There are many ideas to what is happening in your dimension as you access higher dimensions while in your physical bodies. We can tell you this: there is no one set program. The program you have been reading "Stasis Period" is, indeed, a program that is being examined as a possibility of being implemented, but that is yet to be determined.

Q - This Stasis Period says that certain people will be lifted off the planet and this book, The Pump, says that this will not happen. Yet you say that this program is being examined.

A - At this moment, there is no need for such a program. The political unrest coupled with the financial collapse of your present monetary system is awakening people to what is important to them. Yes, many people now live in fear and want to protect their homes and selves with any tool or weapon available. There has been a "need" for many people to purchase guns and ammunition for this perceived protection, as many people, feeling the effects of the increased bodily frequencies, are "freaking out," not being able to assimilate the higher frequencies because of the fears they hold inside of themselves. At the same time, you have people reaching out to one another, holding one another's hand to help them through this process of transformation. Even though most people are unaware of the ascension plan, they are aware they have a compassionate heart, and this heart heals their fears.

Q - A few years ago, I read that the Earth would go through a pole reversal where our Sun will rise in the west. Some of my writings also say that our sun will fade and that our light will come from the Earth herself as well as from us humans. Also, I have read that Jupiter has become our second sun and presently it is behind our solar Sun. What we see as the known position of Jupiter in our skies is actually a large ship taking its place until we, humanity, are ready to accept this second sun and the magnetic pull it will have on our Earth. Please comment on this.

A - You have learned through your writings that your solar system is moving and changing.

Jupiter is one such planet who had made enormous changes. And she has moved her station to one of servitude to Earth as well as the other planets within this solar system and beyond. She shall shine as a beacon to new understandings that are taking place now. She will eventually come out of hiding (from behind the Sun), so to speak, to shine her light, physically and vibrationally. You will definitely see the changes, for they will be immediate. Please do not fear this change. It is for the highest good of the All.

Q - Will Jupiter be our second sun for a short period of time before Earth lets her own light shine?

A - As your solar system evolves, as well as other systems within your galaxy (you effect all other systems), you will find continuing changes taking place. Jupiter will remain a sun to you for many years until the next period. We cannot give you a date for this transition because you will perceive time in a much different way. By the way, your Earth always lets her own light shine, just many do not see it.

Q - Thank you.

A - We are always available to serve humanity and the Earth. Any questions you may have, we are at your service to answer for your better understanding of the processes taking place. We thank you for your thoughts, for they help us understand any misconceptions that you may have. We are your brothers and sisters of the stars. You also know us as the Els of Antarena, an area where you have quarters. *Note this reference to quarters pertains to this author.*

I am still using a lot of discernment regarding Jupiter as our second sun. I have asked about this many times, and I am told that this is so.

August 31, 2009

A Grass Roots Approach

Most of your current world has lived on what is termed a grass-roots approach. A thought comes into being, then man devises the order of progression to develop the thought to manifest itself. This way has served mankind for many millennia. Man has used his hands-on approach (left-brain thinking), to put an order into his wishes and desires. However, the time is short for this approach to be efficient. What is happening on the earth plane is a shift in the way creation manifests itself. Because of the former low-density of the third dimension, man needed this grass-roots approach to manifestation to make sure their dreams made it into their reality. There was what is called lag time between the dream and the end result. This approach worked wonderfully so the human could express his intention through the process. The process was what was important for the human to grow in his intellectual pursuits along with his emotional and physical bodies well attached.

Now what is happening is the intellect is still well intact, but the emotional body is taking the left brain out of control. What that leaves, one may think, is the right brain. But this is not so. There is no right and left brain in the higher dimensions. It is one brain that is the computer control mechanism in the human body. It is attached to the physiology of the body, and also the higher mechanisms in the workings of the total Being. The signal from the major glands, particularly the pineal, is the conductor of magnetism forming a vortex of energy developed into wave patterns, the actual connective tube within the creative force. Picture a matrix over a matrix over a matrix, never ending. These matrices are built into a spiral and there is a connection from one matrix to the next. This pattern is the construction of you, thought arranged in a pattern to be built upon itself yet is a part of the all of you and creation. There always is movement, yet in the lower dimensions, you are unable to see that movement. And that is changing as your consciousness is taking more neutrons, like a base center, for movement within the vortex. These help stabilize the interactions within yourselves, the ability to be fully present in more than one place. Time is not a factor since there is no such thing as time within the vortex of you.

Therefore as your cerebium, a brain as one hemisphere, develops, you will find that your abilities to manifest will become quite different. Lag time will be in the past, as all your mechanisms of vibrating life will be fully in the now, the connections between the matrices realized, thus utilizing that force to produce your thoughts and desires.

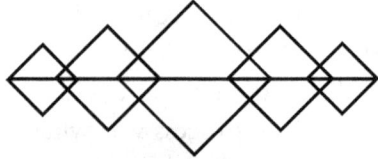

Q – In order for us to see more "movement" within our total self, how does our consciousness take more neutrons?
A – Your consciousness has form, although not a form you can recognize. It is energy arranged in a pattern as spoken above. Therefore, You, as a total composite of your soul or the All of You, are energy in motion. Using more neutrons in this

endeavor enables the many of You (your various incarnations) to enter into any of your crystallized forms (physical and non-physical forms). In your book "Mystery of the Universes" (see Book 44, Book of Anatomy) neutron energy is explained in how it relates to your human body. Now take that concept a little further into the programmed geometries of your soul. The implosions caused from the increase of neutrons on cellular structure enables consciousness to move into other crystallized forms, thus the ability to move that consciousness to anywhere you desire to go. The above writing says that with these connections realized, your thoughts and desires will be utilizing this higher consciousness to create whatever you want in the now.

September 9, 2009

The Uniqueness of You

Each one of you on the Earth plane is unique in your personalities, your physical appearance, and your motivations for being here at this time, or any time in the cyclical process you have here on Earth. What enables you to become One in your conscious understandings is your ability to let go of all the preconceived beliefs left for you from your former existences experienced in linear time. There is no one or no thing that can ever be who you are when you incarnate in physical form, be it in this 3rd/4th dimension, or you in the other realms of dimensional existence. Because of this, you Creator have found that there is no such thing as enforced existence, only your reasons for being in whatever situation, body (life form), or universe, all within the One. Liken this to your fingerprints. There are no two fingerprints that are exactly the same.

As each of you progress in opening up your consciousness levels, you will find that the bigger you has some growing up to do. By this we mean you will always grow in your awareness on some level within you, but the outer awareness only becomes evident when you can see the whole process of creatorship unfold on a conscious level. That is happening now in this new age of understanding. As you grow in your current understandings, you will notice that you have the ability to take a life form, a part of your whole being, and move it into another time and place to become another living aspect in a different setting and circumstance. Why you do this is to widen your perspective of Creator Source in its attempt to realize the internal motion of the Self.

We have come from so many backgrounds of understandings making our moves into the new realms. We are always creating and to be the conscious creator, we are dropping all forms of limitation. What we dream, we create. New forms are always in process. We are incredible!

September 9, 2009

Shifting Sands Through Time

The metaphor, the sands of time, is one to contemplate. Time is not stationary, always moving, morphing in space. You can shift forwards or in reverse. You have the capability of that movement once you understand the physics you call time. It is your belief system on the 3rd dimensional Earth that time continues ad infinitum, and in a way, it does. You now know that life is eternal, that there are multiple dimensions of existence, we all are part of the One Creator, each having our own experiences within and for the One. But what you will be experiencing as you move into the conscious understanding of how life really works with Earth, is your knowledge that what you perceive as time is light changing its focus. It is not that light, the essence of Creator, is directed at you, but by you. Light is also known in your religious circles as the Holy Spirit. It is you who direct this Spirit, and it is you who is Spirit. How you direct this Spirit is totally your search into the unknown, which is unknown until it is created or known by you. You have developed this system called the 3rd dimension so you can understand the simplicity of creating from this Light. Light begets light, and this system revolves within a circle of divine magnetism orchestrated by the forces of the powerful I Am Presence, that which you are a part. It is this power that enables you to dream your dreams into reality. It is not that you are in a stupor manifesting your dreams, but in your awakened state of consciousness.

You are developing a keen sense of knowing that in the forces of the One, you shall take what is made manifest and bring it to an understanding of such a magnitude that you literally are creating a new space and time. It is all in your creating that you manifest new frontiers. And these frontiers are always before you ready for you to take in what experiences you may wish to own. Once you own every experience and be grateful for that experience will you be able to move to new heights within your physical beingness. This is happening now as each of you move into your new frontiers of new life. You do this individually and with one another, as you all play a part in the dream. What you will find is that each one of you in the dream will experience something different. You will witness something totally different than your brother or sister, yet you play together to make your dreams be a reality in the new time and space.

In your conscious understandings, you will notice that your brothers and sisters will all play their parts perfectly. And you will know that you also play your part perfectly. There is only perfection in what manifests from your dreams. You are the makers and coalescers. Therefore, all is divine order because they come from your desires. Be aware of all that is within your thoughts. They are powerful and they are your beliefs. Masters (you all are), any mistake that you feel you make is never a mistake. If your experiences do not mirror what you think you desire, perhaps you shall look very deep within yourself at all your thoughts. Look at any thought that holds you back. You will know what holds you back by the feeling you get in your solar plexus (your gut). You are Source, so you are always connected to that Source which is you. The Source of you is always there ready and willing to communicate with you, the physical being. Therefore, you always have divine guidance and be sure to ask for this in all your thoughts.

As you transcend into the 5th dimension, all thoughts will be pure. By that we mean that all thoughts will be centered where you will no longer have to watch what comes out of your mouths. It will be as a pure essence, unconditional love made manifest.

Your new journey has begun. Your frontiers are now open. What do you wish to project into these frontiers of new knowledge, wisdom, and love?

Time is like sands in your hands. The crystal pebbles roll over your palms, through your fingers. Love every pebble because each one represents you, each one a life mixed together to make up all your lives. They all exist together then fold into the other sparkles of crystalline energy. You are the Masters, this is your playground.

September 11, 2009

The Mountain and the Molehill

Many of you are building mountains, and some of you are building molehills. Both hills are important because they are your creations. If you decide that you want to build something different, then you have that perfect right. It is the right of each one of you to build what you please as long as it does not interfere with anyone else's creation. Does building a mountain seem more important than building a molehill? Does it really matter which you build?

Dear ones, it is totally up to you what you want to build, be, act, dream, or anything else as part of creation. You are the one that is in charge of you. You are not in charge of anyone else ever. This doesn't mean that you cannot be a caretaker. Most everyone is a caretaker some time in each of their lives. It is part of the experience of living. You are only in charge of you!

What we are seeing and witnessing on the Earth plane is the need of many humans to be of service, a more direct way of getting involved. Remember only get involved if invited to do so. You can always ask if someone wants assistance, but if they decline, then stay out of their business! Remember each one of you may only want to build a molehill, or even dig a ditch.

It does not matter in the divine world. There is no one out there that is taking notes on your perceived good deeds, except yourself. The best good deed for each and every one of you is to attend to your own business and love yourself in the process.

I am hearing you ask: "What about those desolate people that live in poverty, in hunger, and disease? What about those who are mentally incompetent and cannot live on their own? They certainly need my help so they can work through the poverty that they live in. Many of those people cannot care for themselves. We need to help and protect them."

Consider this. These people who you feel need your help may definitely need your assistance. What you should be aware of is that you do not have the right to tell them how to live, worship, eat, or any other shouldisms coming from your ego. Volunteer only when invited to do so. If someone wants your opinion, then state your opinion, not your judgments. What is the difference in an opinion and a judgment? An opinion is your point of view on any given subject. A judgment stems from your ego and the ego is saying that 'I know best.' Therefore you want another to react or act in your perceived point of view. How many times have you spoken about a subject, then the person with whom your discussion was with quickly changed the subject? If they are not interested, they will ignore what you are saying anyway. Everyone on this planet has their own agenda.

Those who are deemed mentally incompetent do need assistance. Remember when dealing with these people, they are filling their own contracts. Their gifts are innumerable. They teach unconditional love.

Each one of you is a teacher. You not only teach yourself, you teach others by your example. Before you speak, take into consideration your intent. Everyone has their own story and interests. Listen intently to another, yet allow yourself your own space. You can learn so much by just listening, therefore you also are the student. You all create together, each one of you is unique. And each lifetime is unique.

Appreciate yourself in all of your fullness, and respect others in their own creations. We learn together. Life is so much more interesting when we allow all of us to just Be.

September 16, 2009

Focus

Today as I activated the higher energies within me and invited my guides who want to assist in this writing, I see in front of me a gathering of beings who will act as one voice. It is interesting to "see" inter-dimensionally all the wonderful beings who are with us and a part of us. They are acting as one, therefore they will share their thoughts regarding focus.

It is our pleasure to work with you this day and discuss this word "focus" and what this really means. Most humans use this word often so they can focus their thoughts, visions, and other senses into their intent. In order for an intent to manifest itself on the 3rd-4th dimension of your reality, one must focus on what they want to accomplish. They see with their in-turned eye the end result. We tell you that indeed you see an end result, but most manifestations take turns or other ways to actually manifest, perhaps much different than the perceived way to get there. Remember that one's "there" may be much different than another's "there." So it is interesting to witness the procedures humanity uses to "get what they want."

Even though you humans are a one civilization, meaning that you exist within your human bodies on this Earth at essentially the same time, you each came into this existence to experience the changing of the human form into a more homogenized being. By that we mean that you touch one another more deeply through the energy of your hearts, plus you are tapping further into the wonderful higher You. You are living in a time where you are focusing on the bigger picture and that includes the merging of the physical you into a more realized part of your higher or God Self. We watch with wonder this divine process you have created.

We now notice that as you perform your daily routines, you are reaching further into the consciousness that permits you to see your part in the whole process of this human activation/development. Each of you is becoming more aware of the bigger picture, and you have a big part in that picture. You now know that this is the time of human intercourse into the higher dimensions, an evolvement into the parts of Creator, physical and non-physical. What we are witnessing is this integration, and we see you in a whole new light. You physically glow, actual light, from your physical beings as you hold the love of the higher You.

Your ability to focus gives you the opportunity to receive whatever is your desire. And that desire pulls from the universe what is needed to make any manifestation. Keep in mind that there are now billions of other beings on your planet and off your planet that are focusing on their desires. Because you, in reality, are One, then the energies that make up your manifestations may come to you in unexpected ways. It is because you all are creating together, and together your desires are becoming more homogenized. To truly manifest what you desire, let go of how this manifestation is to occur. Understand that each one of you has unique abilities and in order for those abilities to be used, let the universal energies intermingle so the final result is the best for everyone. Keep in mind that the final results are always changing as you grow within the total You.

Thank you for allowing us to speak to you this day. We are always with you and will assist you only when called upon. We are your brothers and sisters of the stars. We come as one.

September 21, 2009

Flying Colors

It takes courage to understand then act what you feel is in your highest interests. Does that mean that you do only what is for your highest good, always? It seems to us that this world is becoming a beacon for misunderstanding, waving its colors for those to come to your rescue. Is that what you really want, someone to come to your rescue? Why is it that the human has so many problems taking care of himself (or herself)? Why does he need someone to do something for him and then he feels it was done for his best interest? It seems to me, that this world of chaos shall come to an end, an end that shall be no more to allow the human to take himself out of the pressure to do only for others not thinking about himself. So it is this time on planet Earth. What one perceives on this side of the globe, another perceives differently on the other side. Why is this?

Humanity, please allow yourself the privilege of thinking for yourself. Allow others to think for themselves also. Your perceptions may be quite different. You each have your own agendas, and because of that, you will lead different lives. What is important to one person may not be important for another. And that is because you have the different agendas. This world is such an interesting place to be because of the diversity that is exhibited throughout the many cultures living on the surface. Please remember that each one of you have chosen your own life, your life, not that of another. So let them grow, experience at whatever level or degree that is for their own highest good. It may not be for your highest good and it shouldn't be. You each have you own set of circumstances that are in place for you to grow and experience the many wonders of being in the physical body.

This time you call the new era will be a menagerie of cultures coming together to share one another's thoughts. Remember that what pleases another may not please you. Let them have their life so you can have your own. When trying to control another for the sake of feeding the ego self, then you will find yourself living another's life that you really have no interest in living. Work together for the greater good, but allow each one to have their own say about their own life. Yes, there are those cases where one is unable to care for their self either mentally, physically, or emotionally. You do have every right to assist, but only when asked, usually by a family member of the disabled one.

This is a new time and place. The yesterdays are gone and the tomorrows will always be tomorrows. Focus on your own wants and desires. Look at how those wants and desires interface with your loved ones. Support one another. Let them live their experiences without telling another what to do and how to do it. This wonderful ascension plan is at work, and it is working wonders. Whatever you desire in your life, go ahead and focus that intent. Just know that what you desire is for you and only you. When your desires work with another, and they will, know and trust that you will receive magnificent benefits of living and working together. You will know that each one is a brother or a sister. This is life and the way it is.

Give gratitude for your many blessings. They shall flow with ease with only love in your heart. The future will always be the future, so only focus on this very moment. Your moments shall even be grander than they are now. Even those moments you recognize as despair will soon disappear, and the new heavens will make themselves known.

Follow your own hearts. Many hearts will mesh into One, but you shall still live as an individualized heart. The bricks are loosening from the mortar. The many towers humanity has built throughout the ages are coming down. New towers are being built, not out of brick and mortar, but out of stone, rock solid stone, a part of this Earth. You are one, you are One. So be it!

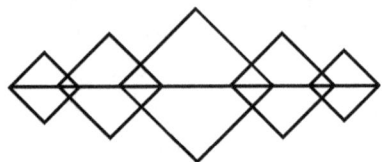

Q – Why is this writing called "Flying Colors?"
A – One meaning (see first paragraph) pertains to those of you who wave your arm or flags waiting for someone to rescue you.

It also means, in a more positive aspect, the following. Each of you has your own set of experiences, hence your ability to tune in to your own particular set of vibrations to accomplish why you incarnated in your body at this time. You create your own ideas of life, allowing your own "colors" to manifest. Allow yourself the love of Creator to become your love in the flesh, flowing effortlessly through you as a bird flies effortless in the currents of your winds.

August 17, 2009

Importance of Art and Architecture

Art in its purest form, that it comes from the innermost being-ness, is a reflection of inner life. It directs and shows the out-turned eye what is within the in-turned eye. It reflects the magnificence of humankind in its endeavor to produce the most immaculate wonders that exist in this universe. When you stop and ponder a piece of art, be it a painting or a sculpture, you find that the piece 'talks' to you in whatever way you are perceiving it. It is showing you something that resides within you, therefore there is a resonance to the piece. What it is telling you may differ from another's interpretation, even the artist himself (or herself). So it is with life, each one has their own interpretation of what they see and feel.

In the field of architecture, many forms are produced using a multitude of materials. Each material used has its own resonance, the energy held within. All materials are energy, and some of the materials used such as rock and minerals have a symbiotic relationship with a human's biology because it is a part of the earth. Information is stored within many minerals. The major one used in building materials is your granites that contain many small crystalline structures of quartz. All quartz crystals have properties that are either transmitters, record keepers, or generators. The use of granite can create quite a symphony of energy wherever it is placed. Because of the other minerals in granite, most stone is very grounding, a part of your Earth Terra. However, pure quartz crystals contain the properties described above and are used within your health systems and technologies that have taken the human's evolution to a technological revolution. The technological applications have barely been touched. You will see that the possibilities with this stone will seem miraculous. You eventually will be able to produce this stone artificially even though the properties will remain organic.

Metals from within Earth's body have been processed to create magnificent structures. The heavier metals such as iron will continue to be used because of its strength. Some of your other metals such as copper will continue to be used within your electrical structures. A new metal will be introduced that will mimic copper with its magnetic flow into electricity, and it will be used to generate a more cohesive display of light without the use of the burning of fossil fuels or the need of the flow of electricity. It will be used in what is termed "free energy." These new inventions that are now taking place on Earth will revolutionize your current system, and man will be able to build beautiful edifices again, as he has in the past before the veil was pulled. The materials used will be looked at with how its properties affect the physical human, the energetic flow within this universe. The details of these edifices will remind humanity of its god self, much more than any great cathedral now on the earth plane.

There are many other art forms expressed in the physical. The art of music touches the inner being with it multitude of resonances and harmonies. It is up to the recipient of music, the listener, to how the music is to be interpreted, for each person's genetic make-up is different. What may be soothing to one may not be soothing to another. Resonance is what makes up the body's biology. Therefore, to interpret for one may not be true for another. Please understand that all music is created for the listener (and the composer) to profoundly affect one's internal structure. There are certain musical scores, that by the most part, sooth one's being or "rev it up." By rev it up, we mean that it causes many revelations and revolutions within the body structure. There also are musical scores that slow down the hyped up processes within the body, and will even slow the heart rate. These relax the body and can elicit the mind to go into a reformed state of consciousness. These reformed consciousness' include a move into one's other states of being in the various levels of life, the multitude of dimensions. Many humans are now using what they call meditative music, music that allows for the conscious to project into other waveforms.

At this time in the evolution of the human body and mind, art is a precursor to the events that follow in the dreams made manifest in the physical dimensions. Realize the importance of such changes going on, and start looking and listening to what artists display for you to grasp or let go of. There is a lot of what many people describe as destructive music, hard rock that disturbs the nervous system. They describe an uncomfortable feeling with the repetition of the lower base sounds, while others turn up the volume to put their being within the sound structure. Again, what certain resonance's are comforting to one may not be comforting to another. Eventually, all hard rock will disappear as the writers and makers of this music will not find that their bodies resonate to the lower vibrations that come from this music. You will find that a new assortment of music will be popular that will tune the body to its desired frequency, for a person to vibrate in the dimension he (she) chooses to be within. With this technology, one will be able to traverse the dimensions with ease.

Please keep in mind that the day you will absolutely remember yourself as the divine essence that you really are, you will remember the infinite opportunities afforded you through the gods of morrow, you within the total You. Namasté.

October 14, 2009

Finance

In your current world, you are finding that your monies systems are being challenged, your means to finance your governments and militaries are coming to a halt. The old means of dependence upon the government to be there for you, in the systems that run the public works, health care, education, supply and demand (yes, there is influence), are being challenged because of the incompetence of the set systems. Not only is this happening within your United States but all countries around your globe. Most of your world is so intertwined in your financial and trade sources, and this will continue. Separation from one another, in actuality, has ended. Isolationism is a concept of the past, not to return. You are finding that humanity on this Earth plane is interdependent. You all need one another, because you all volunteered to be a part of the plan. And that plan is unity – one world. Soon you will realize the plan also includes One Verse, also known as a Universe. And this Universe is a part of the Omniverse. There is no way you cannot be a part of this All.

   Your monetary systems are changing into a new type of system, one that is evolutionary. It is evolutionary in the fact that it includes all world monetary systems brought under the umbrella of Unity, the new way of conducting business through the technical system called computers. Your current monetary systems still include paper dollars and coins, and these systems will evaporate into "not necessary." By this we mean, there will be no need for the physical monetary systems that are now in place. The gold standard has been used, and even this will be discontinued. The replacement system we refer as "Unity" is a system based on equality of production in all countries. This sets up a free will base and equality among governments. The free will equation is the people will decide the "cost" of an item or the "cost" of services. They will set their own fees based upon the cost of raw materials, the amount of work that goes into making an item, and the knowledge to even start a new process. The need for consumer protection will still be there, but only in the sense that a product be thoroughly tested before it goes on the market. What many call inappropriate products or services will be determined by the people. They simply will not purchase a product or service that they don't want or need. What pleases one may not please another. That is what is important in this process of being human, playing inside the biological body. There will be no forced product or service from any government official. The false deities that promote subservience, specifically the male or female in control over another, is breaking down. All people, male and female, are learning to take back their own power, not to give in to false teachings that now are so prevalent upon the Earth.

Your Earth is already a world economic system, but parity among all people will come into focus. No longer will people in one country be able to sell their merchandise or services at an unequal price. There will be those who thrive and those who don't. It depends upon each person in what they want to accomplish while in the human body. The barter system will remain, but it is not a means to "beat" the system. It is a means to accomplish a way to live, specifically working with those in each one's local community. Community will be very important. But also, people will still love to travel to visit the exquisite beauty that is your Earth, and learn from the many cultures. It is such a beautiful blending, a cultural merge in some respects, yet a place where each soul can come to experience just what it means to live in the physical.

This Unity financial system will put all people on equal footing. It is backed by no physical means, but by the attitude and aptitude of all brothers and sisters on the planet. It eventually will work with off-worlders in this exchange of goods and services. Keep in mind that nothing is allowed to be brought to this Earth if it in any way can harm the ecosystems in place. It is fair and just. This is the way of the New Earth.

Thank you for allowing us this time to speak to you about this very important aspect of living on this planet. This Unity system has started and it won't be long before it is fully in place. At first the people will rebel, but then soon will find this solution very workable.

We are known as the peacemakers. We are very much a part of your Earth and planetary systems that surround you. We come in service. We humbly leave to focus on our tasks at hand. Salud.

October 29, 2009

The Current

There comes a time when all shall come to an understanding that this world is coming to an end of an era that has been so phenomenal, so interestingly complete in its knowledge that life in the form of lower dimensional constructs has given such a gift to Creator Source in this Universe. The concept of time has been so well used in that this world called planet Earth could only survive under such conditions. The interesting part of this plan was to bring an understanding to the many cultures, ways of life, in the myriad views of the creators. It has been so complete in the way this plan unfolded, the intermeshing of thoughts and dreams, the technological auspices bestowed upon the forms who bonded with the biological sphere of Gaia. Now the table is turning, using Earth's vernacular. They are turning into another form, yet a part of the total of the One.

The currents of understanding are changing or morphing into a more realized genre of living in the physical. The physical matter that makes up the human and the earth are changing in their frequencies of life and light, the electromagnetic forces coming together in this segment of the universe, the physical universe of the totality of All There Is, yet so beyond the visions of the current humans. Yet, this change or morphing shall only come about with the forces of the Mind, the energy held and connected with the mind of the human, Gaia, and all of the planets and suns that reside in this physical universe. It has been spoken that this transformation shall take place, so this was set up when the Mind decided that all was accomplished as planned.

This current runs through all the collective cords of the All, those collective cords that make up the various matrices of life unending. It is the eternal Mind as One who made the decisions. "Decisions" is only a word used on the Earth plane, yet is closest to what we are sharing with you. It really is not the "decision," rather it is the eternal You coming to an understanding or knowledge in and of itself. There is a Universal Law of the One that says:

In the frequencies that comprise the All, the moving life, the wavicles, a bond enters into another state of existence once a frequency is mastered. It is the physics of life.

So what we are aptly saying is that once humanity on this Earth plane has mastered living in one dimension, actually consciously working with your mind and body's frequencies with the knowledge that you will not and, therefore, cannot devolve, then you go onto another level of frequency.

The current of understanding is also the current that takes you to this "new" place of co-creation. The next level in this co-creative force has always been in existence, yet with the power of mankind in the mix, a new life form is made (you are the makers). Realize that mankind is a composite of many life forms who came to this planet to be a part of her (Gaia) in the physical. She came into the physical also to understand this physical manifestation or low density of frequency. You all, as One, are traveling on to create new worlds of form. Once you cross that matrix beyond the physicality you now enjoy, you will see and feel life force in a whole new way. You will maintain some of your current Earth knowledge, but this current understanding will eventually fade from your beings, not to return. There will be no need for this history, because you will understand time and space to be one and the same. We impart this knowledge so when you make that leap into the New World, you will know that you are not dreaming as you do in your sleep. You will be fully awake, much more so than you think you are now.

Thank you for allowing us our part in this book of writings. Love yourself and love dearly the god that you are. We shall meet with you face to face once you begin residing in The New World. We are your brothers and sisters and we look so forward to our meeting. We do meet on the inner planes, yet when the more of each one of you transforms your self onto this plane, our existence will be so much grander. Salud.

Note: Read Book 80, "The Greatest Story Ever Told" within the first book *Mystery of the Universes*. This writing explains the twelve layers of existence. The understanding given in "The Greatest Story Ever Told" will assist you in understanding this writing.

November 13, 2009

Blue Moon

"Once in a blue moon" has been one of your sayings, and this saying states that something rarely happens. This is the time of "once in a blue moon." What we are stating is that humanity has overcome (have gone beyond) their reasons for the third dimensional shift. Humanity is now living on the boundaries they have set before them to vanquish all that has served them up to this point in their evolvement into the next dimensions of being. The world, Mother Earth, is gaining respect by humanity, something that has to happen for humanity to go further into the higher dimensions. You have learned that humanity and Mother Earth live dependently together. You also have learned that in order for the Earth to move into the New Earth, it must shake off the old patterns humanity has bestowed upon her. That is happening now. There has been some shaking, and this will continue. It may not happen as has been foreseen in your prophecies, because humanity has changed, in some ways slower than expected, and in other ways, faster than expected. What we wish to tell you this day is that the Earth is moving and is moving fast.

This grand movement is part of the plan, Creator's Plan. Keep in mind that you are a part of this Grand Creator, so it is your plan. In so far as we, on the other side of the veil, can see is that this movement that you are a part of is happening at such a grand speed that, indeed, it seems like a blink of an eye that New Earth and remaining humanity will be living in complete comfort, living together for the upliftment of All. What is negligible in this process is the discomfort of humans as they go through the changes. What we mean by negligible, that in reality, it is no big deal. What is a big deal is that this process is happening and it is happening on a grand scale. What may seem like a very long time in the present earth realm is such an infinitesimal point of your overall existence. This is such a small amount of time that you feel the effects of this change, and these changes have not been easy.

The roller coaster ride is almost over. Sure you will have the ups and downs for some time yet, but there will be more ups than downs. In your earthly time line, these changes will continue over the next fifty years, most changes happening now. Most of you will have transcended the third dimension within the next five years. The alignment of your Earth with the center of your Milky Way galaxy is propelling Earth to its new position. You will see the physical changes in your skies, and they will be reflected in Earth and yourselves. These changes have been discussed within your other writings in this book.

The announcement of the new day and time, meaning a new time line, has been established. The Mayans knew of this plus many of your other ancient cultures. Humanity has turned the corner with Mother Earth, and you are soaring to new heights within your consciousness. You are learning of your multi-dimensionality, and it will seem like a whole other life when you start living consciously in multi-dimensions. The term "timeline" will disappear, however, you still will be living in a time capsule, another part of yourselves taking along experiences from your other existences. Thus you are now a composite of the total You, working with other soul families, the new way of being. But do remember that you are a part of a soul family and all soul families are part of Grand Creator.

It will be interesting to see how the new humanity works as a team, along with Mother Earth as the New Earth. This, indeed, is a new day and time.

This day in your 2009, you are seeing lots of movement and movements. The world seems to be in turmoil, humanity not sure what comes next. What this is forcing you, humanity, is to fully live in the present. Sure you can make plans. Do you realize that plans are only a dream? Because plans haven't happened yet. What you set your intention on will manifest. They may result from a plan (dream), and that is because you only manifest your thoughts. Be clear with your thoughts. When you are clear with what you really want your life to be, then it has to manifest. You are the one making all decisions, and your life reflects every decision you make. You shall become more conscious of your every thought as you become more aware that you are your own creator.

Salud!

November 17, 2009

Humanity

The god seed has delivered onto this Earth a most wonderful species known as humanity. These incredible beings have such a grand expression of creation knowing full well that all creation resides in the ethers just waiting for their force to combine and make new creation. It is of utmost importance that humanity continues on their plan to create a new species that shall be the curators of the next wave. By this we mean the overseers of creating through their lens of potential, a spark in the energetic waves that they bring to the land. The land upon which they walk has repositioned herself in the great cosmos to enable the next plan to unfold. In order for any plan to unfold is to allow all thoughts to explode on the horizon. This is also termed the "horizon effect." The word horizon can have different meanings. If it is on the horizon, means the plan will manifest itself. It is rising much like the Earth's sun. Humanity is also rising in its consciousness to notice that it set up this plan. The true mark of any being is to allow the god seed to make itself known, and that is happening on this Earth during the transitional period.

Another part of this "horizon effect" is the ability to bring into the mix of allowing all beings within this humanity to act out their own creations, allowing for the finalization of the plan called The Great Experiment. The seemingly incoherent use of the human body is being shown or demonstrated by the wars, the famine, the hatred, the misuse of Creator's ideas. Creator kind, those who are a part of this process of creating humanity on this Earth plane, instilled within themselves the use of creator power without their use of knowledge of the bigger plan. What is rising on the horizon is this precious knowledge of the human as gods making what they have developed into a new creation, no longer the misfits of the so-called past. They shall terminate the need to live outside of themselves, outside of the knowledge of their own divinity. They shall unwind in their creatorship and lose the knowledge of the forceful gods of yesteryear. The force of one over another will no longer be present on the new Earth plane. What is being created is the plan of immaculate creatorship, each human responsible for the fortification of their very own selves within the bigger plan of creation.

Humanity, in its endeavors to create a utopian society, will understand their abilities of manifestation to the degree of working with one another to create a much larger matrix. This matrix is the form for the electromagnetic frequencies to flow effortlessly connecting one to another on the new earth plane. The frequencies to be brought into this matrix will allow mankind the opportunity to request various forms to create from. To understand this metamorphosis that is available will bring to all of Creation a new understanding of transitioning between dimensions. This is a new day, a new dawn of understanding life, what it means to be creator in the physical. It is indeed a metamorphosis, an allowance program within the reality of truth, an understanding that goes beyond created creation (into new realms). Perception shall change as this allowance program gets underway. The process has started and will continue until Creator knows itself fully. Then creation will take another turn.

Humanity, you have served well using the biology programmed for you to exist in. You have made it possible for these new understandings to take place. Many of you will return to your stations, so to speak, you will return to that knowledge of your being in the many other realms that you have created. This incredible divine plan is now and forever more, into all eternity. There only is eternity, but in the life flow of human life, it is only beginning. The whispers that have gone before you as humanity came into being has set the stage, a new stage for the life force to manifest itself into new understandings.

We honor all who are a part of this process. You have given such wonderful gifts, and now you shall know of these gifts. It is you who have entered into this new horizon of creation. It is you who have taken this plan into more knowledge, thus wisdom of knowing, really knowing your true self. It is almost done. And so it is.

November 30, 2009

The Impetus

Greetings! We gather here to bring you an announcement. And that is we are so greatly encouraged with the progress humanity is making as they make the commitment to bring this world, Earth, to a whole new level. You have not only made the giant leap that was required to take Earth past the point of no return (to the lower dimensions), but have jump started something entirely new to this part of the universe. You ask, what in reality could be new? You have learned that there is only consciousness and that is what makes up all universes. It is the conduit that transforms all matter. The matter is the continuation of the genetic form you call the body human. Yet the form will no longer be what you see in this day and time. It is morphing and attaching itself to the programs designed and now being implemented by the wonderful hierarchy of mastership. We call it a hierarchy only for you to understand the difference from your present form into the new form that you are becoming. There is no looking back unless you want the comparative measures to see how far you have come. If you desire, you can make up your very own time line and then chart the changes you have implemented into your life. Can you see the changes you have made? Now make up a new chart, a line if you will, and leave it blank (no markings on the line). What you perceive as linear will quickly change to life being non-linear.

The whole make-up of humanity on the Earth plane is going through this portal. This portal is not only a portal of new understanding, it actually is a door that you can swing both ways. This means that you can go forward or reverse in what you now perceive as time. You already do this in the higher aspects of yourselves, however, you will be doing this within the new physicality that you are undergoing. We tell you this now so that when this transition occurs, then you will find less misunderstanding to where you think you belong. This grandiose plan you put together, yes you, is you knowing the grandness of your total being. Most the world will know that there is no god outside of themselves. There will be a few sleepers, but they eventually will wake up.

Now the beginning has begun and there is no stopping this process even with the fear that is being pressured upon you with the news media and the movies that are being produced. Soon you will transcend all fear as those who wish to keep you in such turmoil will realize that they, too, are part of this powerful program called ascension. Dear human being, know the ramifications of this knowledge. There is no way you can ever go back to believing that you are soul trying to please an outside god.

We leave you with this knowledge in this day and time for you to understand that the process will never be impeded. It is the time of new understandings for the eliteness of mastership to take place. To be elite does not mean better than unless you choose to see it that way. It is a place where all are considered masters working and playing together on the playground of physicality intermixing with the higher realms of yourselves. The plan is at work and will not stop because creation cannot stop. It just is.

You, the humans, are embarking on the next ship of probability. It is probable yet has not manifested into being. The ties of consciousness have not yet come together for this to take place. You ask what is to take place? Many of you reading this know about your lightbody or light ship called the merkaba. Soon you will using these ships in your everyday activities. As you integrate the higher aspects of what is now unconsciousness but soon will become very conscious is the eternal aspect of the whole you. This will give you the means to integrate within your body structure the ability to move your body's meridians into a place or position that you will be able to receive the impulses from your higher self and download them into your body. You are being reworked or rewired so to speak. You now know that your pineal gland is becoming more crystallized and other glands are doing much the same. This crystallization is not from anything that you physically ingest or breathe into your body. It is you connecting and materializing the higher octaves of vibrations to move the physical into a receptive vehicle. It is much like your technological devices that receive and give out signals. However, the body's ability far surpasses any technical device.

These light ships or merkabas will serve you in many ways. They will catapult you into new arenas of understanding where you will learn what you have forgotten. They will reconnect you to the many other aspects of yourself and will give you the means to travel through your skies, into wormholes into other universes. It really is an amazing process as you move through the mazes of reality. Hang on to your hats as you fly about. There is help much like your school's teachers and guides. You may receive a list of classes, and these guides will help you find those classes. There will be no getting lost with the help of these guides. The nervous fears of yesterday will be gone.

Another understanding we wish to impart to you this day is that your ability to move about will give you a whole new perspective on what it means to be in the physical. You will find that this experience has given you angel wings, an initiation into flight training. You along with millions and millions of beings traversing the skies of eternity moving about to initiate new ideas, relive old ideas if you want, or go on to start new colonies of creation. We don't want you to get ahead of yourselves (not possible anyway), but do know that you have reached a new plateau of the real you. You were born into this time and place to bring a higher understanding to creation. This knowledge is within you, within every cell of your body. It is pushing you to new perceived heights. It is the impetus to create the next you.

December 4, 2009

The Time of Remembrance

This day, today, is the moment that all shall shed their clothing of deceit. There is no hiding the true deliverer of mankind into the sanctuary of the divine. The savior that is so worshipped is the one who shall leave the mark of ignorance in the files of the new day. It is this moment that shall toss away the old ideas of separation of the divine from the holiness of mankind. Is it not by creed that man shall live forever? Is it not by divine knowledge that man shall shed the skin of the deceitful one? Is it not by the love of Creator that man shall know that it is his right to fulfill the shoes of the deliverer? It is, my friend, that the deliverer is you, who has worn sheep's clothing to hide the very love that made you manifest. It is the creed you decided upon when you agreed to come into being on the great planet of separation. That separation is over and you shall know the wheat from the shaft. These are biblical words that you may be familiar with, however, turn over in your sleep and know that you have left to your own endeavors the countless lifetimes where you slumbered. You now know why you have slumbered. You can feel the newness of the exalted you. How does it feel my friend?

You have heard this word – remembrance - understanding that you were asleep. You are asleep no more so no need to hide in your sheep's clothing. Stand naked in the light of the most radiant One and know that it is you that is the light. Even though you have heard this many times before, do you now understand and know who you truly are? We can see the light is not yet fully on, but do not despair because your light is becoming brighter and brighter. Can you see the changes that have occurred within your being? The light quotient has changed and will continue until you become the great ball of light, a sphere of unparalleled beauty.

My dear friends, you indeed have made it through the most difficult stages of your physical lives. And you are not done yet. It is a process, one that you will cherish forever. This program you put into place has been such an experiential program of determination within the confines of the lost knowledge (also known as the fall of mankind). Can you now claim the beautiful you? Or do you still hide within the clothing pulled over your face? It is time to let yourself know, really know, the magnificence of man, your being a part of this process. Be the authentic You! Do not hesitate to speak your truth. It is time for others to listen so they, too, will know their part. Leave tidbits of information, much like your story of Hansel & Gretel, leaving bread crumbs in their path so they know how to find their way back home.

There will be many more bread crumbs on mankind's path. Stay tuned to the announcements made by your scientific researchers, your archaeologists, those who explore the oceans' depths, and those who study your rock formations. You will soon know many more truths that have been hidden from you. No longer will the main populace of this Earth have their heads in the sands, for they are quickening. They will be ready for answers, in fact, will demand them. And it is you, our dear friends, who shall be ready to answer those questions. You will know what to say, how much to say. Don't worry about your appearance – you will be understood by most. Those who wish to remain as skeptics are not ready to take on the new clothing of light. That is okay, because they are where they need to be.

Be the light. Be the shining example. Be the fornicator of the new mankind realizing the light of God that all inhabit. We thank you for all of your knowledge that is being put forth in this new day. Namasté.

December 29, 2009

The Works

Trust. Trust in the power of You. Trust in the power of God, for You and God are One and the same. Until mankind understands his true divinity, there will continue to be distrust on this earthen plane. It is up to each and every one of humankind to change his thinking and understanding. The time of change has been here for many years, but most people do not see it. They are expecting a chariot to come from the clouds, one to save them from a figment of their imagination, thus their truth. The stories are told over and over again, then they become the truth. And they are the truth, only for those who believe it as so. There are others of you who understand the human species each of you incarnated into. They came to spread the knowledge and wisdom of God within. And they are each and every one of you who read these words. This transformation that is occurring on Earth will change the knowledge and wisdom of those who expect the chariot to descend from the clouds. Little by little, people are starting to see some startling changes, most in your economic and world leadership specters. They are starting to see that the world will never go back to the way it was. They feel that the world is becoming a very dangerous place to be.

But we say it is not dangerous! There is no such thing as danger from our point of view. There are changes and each one of you is in charge of your own changes. The news you see on your television sets show war in many countries, suicide bombers, famine, terrorism, and disease. Yes, these exist in your world, but there is no need for such malarkey. This world is coming to an end, and these old patterns will not be a part of the new earth. There is plenty of substance for everyone on this earth. Remember that you create your own realities and it is time to change your thinking of lack. There is no such thing!

As you move on in your transcendence, you will notice the old patterns disappear. The new You awaits your return to your place in your cosmic family. You have not really left, but your consciousness did not let you know that you a part of a very large cosmic family. Now that consciousness is letting you see these other parts of you and family. In fact, you will begin to acknowledge these other parts of yourself as you integrate them into full consciousness. An enlightening prospect, indeed!

The new wave that is upon you shall break down the barriers you had erected and they are falling at a rapid pace. The new world is already here and you are getting glimpses of it more and more each day. That is how this world works. You had succumbed to a very dense dual world, forgot your divinity, and now have started to return to the focus of love to dispel anything you now see as negative. The new focus will be your ability to know and understand the human as a way to know the forces of magnetic resonance that connect everything as manifested light. It is your ability to maneuver these forces for the benefit of yourself as well as all humanity and this earth. You will change your focus to the knowledge of discipline, the ability to remain in the balance of love. It is not difficult to do this. It is only the natural way of being.

We feel that this writing is important for you, dear human, to understand that the new world is anything but difficult. Release the importance you put into feeding your ego self. The ego will support you but in a much different way than you now experience it. It is there for you to know the processes of life yet not take over in the discipline of obtaining material goods. Know that an exciting world awaits you. It definitely will not be boring, but an exciting place to play as you move into your new bodies.

Please understand the significance of what we tell you. Remember, just remember the time when you were a small child with stars in your eyes as you watched the squirrels and other small animals play in the trees. They were funny little creatures just being and playing their lives. You shall do the same.

January 3, 2010

Lying in Wait

In these times called the new millennium, humanity will find that the degree upon which they determine their life lessons has to do with the amount of tragedy and euphoria they experience. This is what has been referred to as karma. The balance of life in this sphere of multiple life streams has the connection to the foundation of frequencies translated into kinship within a single plane of understanding. Life in its simplest form is in the waves that have been translated into biological frequencies that play upon themselves as they develop new ways of living life that eventually will override the need for time integration. The explosion of substances brought into the physical is the effect from the causal manipulations of the mind of the gods. These manipulations bring together the spheres of knowledge that transpire from the worlds of chaos, or worlds of non-form. This world of form is one world that shall not stand alone in its endeavors to develop the human from the seeds of the many worlds who have come to this place and time to assist in this creation. The activity, or action plan, was developed to bring a new course to build upon, new inventions, new ways of being, new patterns derived from the simplistic form of the atom.

The new understanding that the human seed will experience is in the modules or sections of forces, the mind-control mechanism established for humanity. It is humanity that lies in wait for the new stream to take effect. It is the patterns of creation transforming from the waves or intentions of the humans. This patterning is developed from the roots of all dimensions, the One Creator set up in this quadrant of physical manifestation. As the seeds germinate, the flower of life will take on new form. It is in the cones that spell out the next formation. It is a calling much like the cones used at the sporting events that take place on the present (or what feels like the present) earth plane. The development of the new human has been germinating since the birth of this Earth, the time of solar formation to bring about new life. The sun or sol (soul) of this solar system shall be known as the grand gateway. It is through this gateway that man will know himself not as a human but a grand being.

The wait is almost over. The sun shall leave its position, the sol's planets shall take on a new glow, and the movements made by all planets and their moons shall commence. This bountiful Earth shall reintroduce herself as a great player in this game called living in the moment. The firmament of Earth is changing its structure. The waters are moving and settling in new places. New lands are rising. New elements are making themselves known because of the change of physics happening when there is a dimensional shift. What once was a toxic element will no longer be toxic to the new human. The effect of what has been called negative thought will not touch the beauty of this new form, therefore negative thought will not be a part of the new world. It is through the development of the new species that will catapult this solar system into the new place or position to be the grand leaders for the new worlds of form.

Ask yourself the one question that has been in your mind since you were a small child. Who is God? God is and ever shall Be. God is, therefore We are. Our creations are our makings and we shall create together, together with all of our families from far away galaxies and our families who live with us on this planet. Those who have left their human bodies but stay within the ethers of this planetary system will come home with those of you still in physicality. The merging of the dimensions, connecting the life forms to once again communicate through the forces of the mind. The mind is taking on new form to hold the new patterns of creation. You witness these changes in the children as their knowledge is still intact when they enter into new forms.

Look out onto the horizon and notice the changes all around you. The sky is changing in color as the brighter hues emanate from Earth's body. The yellows and oranges are becoming brighter, the greens of the plants look even more intense yet restful as they reach toward the light of sol. The depth of the blue sky goes on into eternity or so it seems. A new color in your skies will become apparent in the coming days, and that color is fuschia. The solar flares coming from sol are penetrating through your atmosphere. This is nothing to fear, only embrace these changes.

The new day is here. The New Earth awaits your arrival, yet you wait until the rest of the world catches up. Do not tarry, no need to wait. Live the wonderful life that each one of you so skillfully developed into Being. Let go of the old patterns of creation as these are fast fading as the new patterns take hold. Behold the new world. Our grand lady is changing her inner form, what you know as inner Earth. Her seed has sprouted and the human will be able to hear her new song. It is a tune and a most pleasing tune that you will never tire of. Be at peace, be at peace. Namasté.

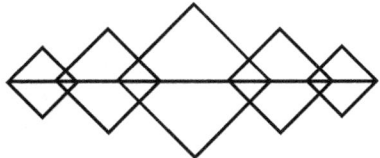

Q – In the second paragraph, it says our new understanding we will experience is in the modules, the mind-control mechanism established for us. I understand we are moving into a new capsule, another part of ourselves taking along experiences from our other existences as explained in Book 64, "Blue Moon." The above writing says that the mind-control mechanism was established "for" us. I feel that is was established for us by us. Please comment.

A – Since you are a part of Creator Source, of course You are making these decisions, that is, the You as your Higher Self or God. You, as a third dimensional human because of your denseness seen as separate from this Source, do not have the capacity to make these decisions consciously. Therefore, the higher aspect of each of you combined has come up with the decision to move forward or ascend this third dimension. Thus what is called mind-control, in reality, was established by the all of You and that is to continue creating with more aspects of yourselves. You are not being manipulated by anyone, only merging with more of yourselves to create new worlds.

February 10, 2010

Beyond the Material World of Temptations

The new day dawns. It shines brightly into all the crevices left from the old world. The crevices are no longer hiding the secrets of the old world. They are no longer hiding the pockets of misinformation left by those who sought control of the populace. These ones (who sought control) are leaving their posts they voted themselves into. What once worked for them no longer holds the power they once took for themselves. There are a few that are trying to hang on to their control mechanisms, but their grasp is slipping. This will leave you, mankind, to consciously make decisions that will not only benefit yourselves, but all of mankind. Humanity, it is your right to think for yourselves. It is your right to do what is best for you. When you do only what is for your best interests (highest good), then those decisions will be also for the highest good of all. It can be no other way. What comes from your heart comes from Creator.

These times of transition will catapult you into the new human. We have discussed the many changes that you will go through, but we have not given you all of the information. The light that you are will start to show much like the paintings of old which show a halo of light around the anointed ones.

Yet this light will not only emanate from your heads, but your entire bodies. It is physical and also a metaphor. Jesus is called the Light of the World. We say to you, you all are becoming the Light of the World. All shadows are being illuminated. Look at your lives and see those shadows you have yet to embrace. Some of them have been hidden for many lifetimes, yet they have brought you to this auspicious time and place. Look deeply at these illumined shadows and note the discipline you took or need to take to overcome such illusions. Are there not lessons left in these shadows? Overcoming your greatest fears will totally free you from all previous ties. Ask (your guides) that you be shown your fears. Be not afraid. Know that when these fears are embraced for what they truly are, they will fall from your shoulders. There is no need to continue carrying them with you.

You will enjoy such profound freedom. Freedom has always been yours yet you succumbed to a denseness to find out how to live in such a dual world. Absolute balance is returning to the earth plane. You have devised such a device called the balance weight or scale, putting gold on one side, and your aspirations/actions on the other side. Gold represents purity. Actions come through the heart, and anything that comes through the heart is always pure. The ego mind is letting loose its grip. The material world of temptations is part of the fun being in the material world, yet do not let it run your life. The ego does not play the heart. Live in balance. See the scale level on both sides.

Action then comes through the workings of the heart. It will propel you into new worlds, some familiar, others not familiar. We tell you this: you will not be disappointed entering the new worlds. We look forward to visiting with you face to face, much like in your current world. Many of you now see us through what you call your third eye. Your third eye, through the workings of your pineal gland, will open new vistas and you will have no doubt that you will be in our presence and we in yours. It is exciting for us here. We shall walk together, dine together, and make love through our hearts.

It is only when you are ready to step into your new positions that we will take your hand and help you through the gates. The gates are pearly glistening light emanating from you and we. It is divine. Let us be together as we create new worlds of love.

Namasté.

We are Lucas, Joseph (Coat of Many Colors), Mary Magdalene, Kryon, Michael, and Rameses. We are known as the Lords of Light. Come join us.

February 19, 2010

From Whence We Shall Come

It has been a rocky road for many of you as you go through the transition of becoming a galactic human. The fast approach of the new Earth has already made a statement to the humans. Humanity has shown their resilience and continues to show their power as they learn that all power is in their hands. It does not matter where their hands have been. It does matter where their hands are Now! To understand this statement, many ones are realizing their connection to all ones on this earth and the Earth herself. The understanding of their true identity as Ones of God are making the inroads into consciousness. This understanding has catapulted mankind into the new way. "Seek and ye shall find" is a phrase given mankind long ago. We tell you that many men are still seeking, trying to find out what life is all about. They look for it in a book, and we tell you it is not in any book including this one. It is in your own person.

    The recordings of long ago hold many truths, but many of the truths were for that day and time. As you progress in your understandings and knowledge of the divine being that you truly are, you will find that inner sanctuary of peace. It has been within forever, because of the foreverness of God, each of you is an integral part of the whole. Please understand this message so that you can go on to new places that you make for yourselves through this power that you are. This is the time, the moment that you have sought for so many lifetimes. It is here and now! It is up to you to start living those dreams that you have so safely hidden.

A saying was given to this author and it is one that shall be repeated here for each of you to recite to yourselves daily. Please understand its significance. It is simple yet has the power to transform the old thought patterns.

Peace eternal
Peace eternal
Peace resides in me eternally

To this day, each of you has said that you want peace not realizing what is peace. To define peace is difficult for most of you, yet such a simple way to be. Peace is:

- A clear understanding of the divinity that you truly are
- Absolutely no judgment by anyone, anywhere, anytime. Judgment is a word that will fade from your vocabulary and thought patterns.
- Joy
- Wonder
- Wisdom wrought from knowledge
- Anticipation brought on by your dreams
- Harmony

It is only through your own heart that you will feel the peace that is yours, and always has been yours. You have tramped through a many wilderness looking for the magic of life. And now you have found it never apart from you. How wonderful is that?

The pace of life on planet Earth has speeded up, or seemingly so. The many changes taking place in and on this planet are moving man into the knowledge of Heaven, that it can be experienced right here on Earth. It is not out there as a place to go when you leave your bodies, but it is a state of being. It is peace.

In this current age as each one of you move from the 3rd density of duality into the higher states of consciousness/being, you have learned a valuable lesson that life is whatever you dream. You have always been the dreamers and always will be the dreamers. Dream big has now been repeated in your airways. Each one of you describe "big" in your own way. There is no right or wrong, there just is. Living in your dreams is what manifests them. You are "there," "here," always in this moment. To truly get a grip on manifesting your dreams is to live them by appreciating every aspect of your life, all of nature, all of the beauty that surrounds you. It is a state of grace given you. Lack, therefore, will fade from your consciousness. It is in the wanting that you are saying that you are lacking.

We share with you this day for each one of you to take your own power and use it for your benefit. Once you live totally in your own power, you will also live gracefully and graciously with all others, no matter their station in life. Yes, you are divine, you can be no less.

Namasté.

February 24, 2010

Foreverness

After reading the writings here set in this book, you now have an understanding of the complete divinity of your being. It is through this vessel, called the human, have you begun to show just how impeccable life is. This vehicle that you have chosen to introduce in the world of form has been the most incredible experiment in the total process of living life. It has given you the tools to process new life and life forms in the ever-increasing manna, the physical aspect of Creator. The bridge between the physical and non-physical remains, however, the way life manifests physically has, indeed changed. It is through the efforts of you as human that this bridge has been redesigned. The auspices of experiencing karma, a tooth for a tooth as told in your Bible, has been a tool that was set in place by the ones of many dimensions – You! And now this tool is receding in its effectiveness as the human takes on new coats of color. Cause and effect, the basics of karma, shall continue because that is how creation works. It is through your efforts of thought, does action come about. This is the only way the material universe comes about.

The formation of the new human is happening now and at a very fast rate, were you to measure time/manifestation. Your perceptions of manifestation in time will change. You are moving into a new sphere of thought. Your comrades, those working with you from the so-called higher dimensions remain in their positions to be of service to each and every person that lives on the Earth. They will continue in this position until each and every Earth human has taken their walk into the new forces of being. Those that wish to remain in the old paradigm will do just that to work and plan their evolution outside the New Earth. They will leave this earthen plane to continue their processes, until they are ready to move forward in their evolvement. We all need them just as much as we need each and every one of you. We cannot be Whole without all of our parts. Please release all judgments on those who wish to remain in the old paradigm. They are doing what they need to do, just as those of you who have chosen to continue in your ascension process. Gratitude is given to you all.

What we wish to inform you at this juncture is that the doorway is closing for those of you who want to ascend. At this time, there is very little time. Either you leave or you move on. Most decisions have been made and all decisions have been honored. The exercise of coercing another's choice through the use of fear will rapidly fade as this tool does not work in the higher dimensions. Remember what you have built just to get here on the Earth at this moment. Each of you chose to be here now and each of you was allowed to be here – by the Higher Self of each and every one of you. There is no one that is allowing you to pass through or holding you back except You. There is no hierarchy.

There will continue to be more Earth changes or alterations so that Gaia (Earth) will of better service to those remaining evolving humans and the Earth herself. Gaia has many tools that she has used to benefit herself, but has held back using some of those tools so as not to harm her beloved children. That time is up as she needs to shed some of the dense pockets of energy left by those who have raped her body. With the help of the Sun and the other planets within this very solar system, will she move to benefit the all. Know that no one is being punished for his or her misdeeds, however, Gaia needs to breathe fully for her to take on her new presence. Allow her to do what she must do for truly she is a gift to each and every human.

This process of life as you transcend the shackles of duality will break forth the bright light of the New Day. Light used in this instance is that glory of being in what many of you call Heaven. No, the streets will not be paved in gold, but life will be golden. It is in the remembrance of the totality of Being knowing life will continue forever more. It just is and always will be.

Q – In the above writing, our Sun and other planets within our solar system are assisting Gaia in this transition. Please further explain.

A – It is with pleasure that we explain this more fully for you. Your Earth, the body of Gaia, is very much a part of your Sun and the other planets that revolve around your Sun, the central core of your solar system. Each planet has their own mission as they, too, evolve just as each of you are evolving. Your planets work together in such a fashion that they connect their energetic corona through the electromagnetic portals, interdimensional portals, to this galaxy, onto the Great Central Sun, where Creator energies originate. They are part of the overall matrix of your current civilizations, past and future civilizations. Everything, all, is connected. Therefore they play an integral part of the distribution and manifestation of all life in this solar system. Not all life is human, plant, or animal. There are many other forms of life that you will connect with as you transcend this heavier 3rd dimension. You are seeing this in many of your photographs taken with your digital cameras. Many of you call these life forms orbs, however, they are not only spheres of consciousness, they can take on other forms not known to you yet. Most 'orbs' are part of your elemental kingdom, but not all. Remember that you as human beings look like orbs from those watching from the higher dimensions. As your perceptions change, will your physical world look different. It is part of the process that you are going through as you traverse the 3rd dimension into the $5^{th} - 7^{th}$ dimensions. Your world appears it is changing, but most of the change is due to your new perceptions.

For more information on our Sun, see Book 60, "Book of Gibraltar, Part 2" in Mystery of the Universes.

March 2, 2010

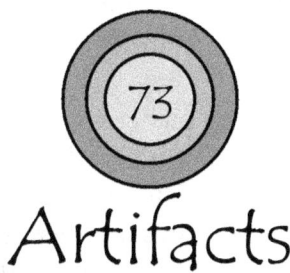

Artifacts

At this moment, your Earth is coughing and leaving off gases in pockets within her. She releases her gasses as she belches remnants of past civilizations not yet known to man in this present moment. What mankind will discover is that many civilizations have existed on and inside of this planet. Some of these civilizations were discussed in the first book "Mystery of the Universes." However, many more have existed and remnants of those people will soon be discovered. Man will find out that not all sentient beings were humanoid. Many have taken on various forms during their lifetime on the earth. All came from other planets and planetary systems, thus they had to change some of their features to accommodate their form on this planet. Take for instance the beings you know as your dolphins. They came here to this planet to assist in the changes promised by the Grand Creators before these Grand Creators could occupy the human form. Thus they came to balance the waters and the lands with their energetic blueprint to bring about a climate that is hospitable to the human form that was about to enter this realm. They helped set up the current eco system, and in order for that to happen, they had to change their form from living on land to living in the waters. What current man will discover are artifacts of the Dolphinian land civilization including drawings/carvings, pots decorated with various motifs, tools, buildings, and vehicles used. This finding shall be startling to most people, yet a memory will surface to many who lived within these communities. The Dolphinians were just one civilization man will soon discover that lived on this planet.

Man, understand that you have had many predecessors and most of them do not look like you. Many have come and gone leaving their footprints to be found. As you may have read in "Mystery of the Universes," this day there are many beings that live in your waters as well as inside the Earth's mantle. Some of them are surfacing as Gaia changes her form to accommodate her new body into the higher frequencies of being. Many of these beings decided to live within the Earth Mother, Gaia, because it better suited their forms. Now they must leave their pockets and enter into this "outer" world. You will find that many of these beings are very advanced in their technologies. Many have flying ships you may know as UFO's. These ships are not from "out there," they are from your own planet! Many of these ships, in various sizes and shapes, will make themselves known within the next few years. Some of them have already been seen and have communicated with various surface dwellers. They will be introduced to this outer world by someone in government within this United States. Other ships will be seen in other places around your Earth. Some will stay within Earth's hemispheres until they feel they are safe to be sharing the surface you all enjoy. Be not alarmed at their appearance. You all have much to learn from one another.

Ancient libraries are being unearthed at this time. The findings, the artifacts within these libraries will be astounding as man will learn that his technology he enjoys this day has been used in many past times. The New Earth will again realize what a gift humanity has been and continues to be. And humanity will again realize just what a gift Gaia's Earth has been to bring creation to such a moment.

It is time for man to put down all of his weapons, as they will be of no use in the near future. Man knows that something is going on, but most do not understand just what that is. It is those of you who do understand this ascension process to be of service to those who are frightened.

Yes, it is this moment that man shall understand their true nature and that is love. There is no one that will punish them in the so-called afterlife. Life always continues, just one stage to the next. Some stages can be repeated and man has known this as reincarnation. Reincarnation as it has worked in the old Earth is also changing as man delves deeper within his own being realizing that it is he who is god creating his own life force. The tentacles have pierced the old form, and the new form is emerging out of its cocoon into the new human, god in perfect form through each one of you. What a delight to witness such grandeur. Humanity, you indeed are going where no earth human has gone before. It is your time because you have made it so. It is up to you to take the reins and transform your new home into the new heaven. Know that you are so much more than just this body. You make up such a complex of beingness, it brings tears to our eyes. We know who you are. No need to introduce yourselves. We are your brothers and sisters, a very intricate part of you, yet we can see you with different eyes. We can see your light as it shines brighter and brighter illuminating the New Earth, a star being born.

Note: Many of the writings in the first book, "Mystery of the Universes," refer to the major planetary systems who all had composed their efforts in the making of many earth forms, including the human. Also see Book 50, "Book of the Nightingale," a writing on inner earth beings and their story; and Book 51, "Book of the Assembly," about The Tall Ones from inner earth.

Many years ago, I channeled a being who called himself Adolphus. Using my inner sight, Adolphus was a large bipedal being who looked much like the dolphins of today. Going back to some of my channelings, I came across the following received on 6-19-2000 regarding interesting information on the inner and outer church, something that keeps coming into my mind and I want to share with you:

"I asked Sananda *(the cosmic name of Jesus)* about The 40 Pillars of the Church, the inner and outer churches. He said it has to do with balance. I said John has to do with the inner church and that John was the name known during the life of Yeshua (Jesus). Sananda said John is Adolphus. John's "church" had to do with love and compassion. (John worked closely with Mother Mary.)"

From Sananda:

"The cetaceans came to earth as the caretakers. They hold a resonance that emanates from the heart. It is their time to relinquish this position and let humanity take over as caretakers. What this means is that we (humankind) must think and act with the heart – love and compassion frequency emanations. [During the time of Jesus] John (Adolphus) could not bring the frequency in to full balance because humanity was not ready to embrace this concept."

"There are 40 distinct races on and in this earth. Each was seeded by four major star systems. Each went out to experience that part of God Creator that needed balance – duality brought together to create a spark, a newness."

The 40 distinct races are also called the 40 Pillars of the Church, church meaning physical vessel. The inner church is the true consciousness teachings - we are a part of God or Creator, and the outer church represents the teachings - God is separate from us (also known as the Church of Peter) which are still popular today. Note that John and Adolphus are both incarnations of one soul. Adolphus is from Sirius. I was also told that the major essence of Sananda is also Sirian. They work closely together.

I also found this message given me by Adolphus on 12-24-2001. Per Adolphus:

"You awaken to the Spirit of the oceans. We welcome you in the Spirit of the One. Our mission, almost complete, was to hold the pattern of divine energy to move through the layers of Baal – that denseness of being that we all volunteered to experience. This weight or heaviness of being was certainly a challenge yet gives that part of Creator Source an added dimension of the total being."

"You are now seeing out of this field into the field of free flow of Creator energies, of Creator manifestation. The sparkles of the new playing field fill your eyes. Ask for them to join you. Your visions shall expand. We, dolphin Sirians, open the fold of energetic fabric and release the hold of the third dimension. You will sail to parts unknown, yet there will be a familiarity."

March 3, 2010

Recall

Once you have awakened from your deep sleep will you realize the lie you have been living. This lie was arranged by each one of you so you would not know the true divinity of your being. In doing so, you have learned much about separation, not only from one another but from your perceived God. This experiment was planned so you would learn what it is to be divine. When you are living in that state of ecstasy, you do not realize that state until you no longer are living in that state. So your experiment began and was orchestrated by each one of you. Otherwise you would not be incarnate at this time. You allowed others to control you, and you did so happily. You allowed others to block your consciousness so you would forget. You allowed others to torture you, or so you thought as you went through such carnage. And now you are allowing yourselves to remove those thoughts and feelings to escape from your being leaving the love that has always been there.

Soon you will recall why you made such decisions. And you will recall the divine essence of your being. For many of you, it is still difficult to fathom such a scenario. You are saying, "Am I nuts?" No you are not nuts. This allowance program brought you to a new place of understanding and you are being applauded for your choices. "What is next?" you might ask. What is next? It is solely up to you for your expansion to take place. Knowledge starts with realizing the grandness of your being. Then you take this knowledge and bring it into all you do in your daily lives. Live love in everything you do and say. Live that happiness you so desperately ask for. It is in the writings that you shall rise up out of the ashes to take back your own power. Now is that time.

Living and breathing your truth will set you free, free from ever questioning your choices, free from ever needing the word forgiveness, and free from any oppression you have allowed to get to where you are now. Are you getting this? Are you allowing this to happen? We say this can be a slow process as all of your earthly lives are merging together to release you to understanding your divine presence. It is happening and the pace is being quickened. You have prayed to your brothers and sisters of the stars. Please hear your prayers and understand what you are praying for. Always ask that you receive whatever is for your highest good. What you have prayed for has not always been what is for your highest good. Please listen to yourselves. Ask for guidance. You will always receive it!

Believe in this change that is taking place. We see some of you going forward, then slipping back a little. We laugh when we see this happening, because of your own self-deprecation. Get over it and move on. Release all that serves you not! We will take your hand and assist you through whatever process you need to go through to truly dislodge any blocks that you still hold on to. The ego is being challenged as you release the need to be right or wrong (it is only balance), rich or poor, the need to be loved. You are always loved, and the biggest block to remove is that feeling of need.

Instant recall may happen to some of you. You will look in the mirror and not know the person staring back at you. Something has changed. Do not let this frighten you. Know that you have released, albeit not always consciously, many of those things you no longer need to live the life of love.

You will get it when you allow yourselves this knowledge to become embedded within. You will become a walking, talking encyclopedia, and you will have the wisdom to know how to use this encyclopedia.

So what do you chose? Do you really have a choice? You always have a choice. That is the free-will aspect of being human. And now is the moment to allow the changes to happen. Just breathe in love, exhale, breathe in again, exhale, and breathe in again. Know the power that you wield, power for your very own selves in the wisdom of choosing love. Once you live this love, the frequencies extend out to all you meet. And you meet everyone on this planet because you are all connected. The velocity of the frequency of love will catapult you into ecstasy once again, but this time with the knowledge of your total divineness.

Know that this time in your evolution, the necessary planetary changes are also taking place. At this moment, your Earth is letting off pockets of dense energy that have held her back. She will continue with this expulsion until she is balanced within her own skin. You will be able to chart these changes and know where her next expulsion will happen. (Note that at this time of this writing there have been recent earthquakes in Haiti, Japan, Chile, and Argentina.) You will also witness bursts of light in your skies, some of them emanating from your Sun, as she too experiences her changes. Your Sun has been called a "he" as well as a "she." It matters not, because it is neither. "She" can be nurturing as well as "he" can be demanding.

Be easy on yourselves as you go through these processes of change. Be loving and nurturing as a mother, yet firm in your commitment to allow the necessary changes to take place. Within this process of recall, you will remember all you need to remember when you need to remember. And so it is.

March 5, 2010

Words

Words are a means of communication, from one human to another, from human to animal, and from animal to animal including your bird kingdom. Human's words come in many, many languages. What is perceived in one language as an adjective may be a verb in another language. The roots of language come from the many ancient cultures who manifested their own sounds from their ancestors, mostly from other worlds. This may be confusing for many to digest, but the human race has evolved as a race, a one race from the many worlds. Each world brought with them sounds particular to their form. The evolvement of sounds, i.e. words, is a mixture of these worlds. You could say that the Earth is a melting pot of many civilizations.

Some sounds resonate a familiarity to humans, each human responding differently to each sound. And that is because deep down within, a particular sound brings up deeply stored memories within the form and energy of the body. The voice, that great tool of the body, speaks loudly to the being emanating the words. It is through this mechanism, the voice, which shall transcend the differential of the species into a more harmonized vehicle. It is happening now on this earth plane, and it will continue as humanity comes about in its directive of usurping the old leagues of active intelligence, those choosing to stay away from the injection of the heart. The ones choosing to live with these changes into the heart shall also change the use of the voice. It is through this divine mechanism that man shall have total recall into the archives of yesterday. Yesterday is only a perception. Each day is new, building on one another, allowing the message to come forth. What this means is that there is the reversal of energy into a form that is rarely used on earth by humanity, and that form is much like your bird kingdom, singing messages about life and the current of the now. So it is imperative that man understands these changes since certain words will recede from their consciousness.

And so it is, the new song shall rise as the eagle its wings[1], as spoken from one of your Native American elders. It is a new voice and this voice shall connect man to be more in tune with his animal and bird friends. You all work closely together as you maneuver out of the third dimension into the fifth dimension. The sounds of creation will come as a thief in the night as you awaken to your new abilities. Do not be alarmed as you hear the quantum calls from your innermost being. It is you emerging from the cocoon of forgetfulness into the new realm of manifestation. Your music, ones made through your instruments and the instrument of your voice will be like a new toy to be played with. Together you shall resonate to the upper dimensions of your soul, the living God that you are.

The seven-note scale that you are familiar with will increase as you soon will hear sounds not yet known to you. Your musical scale will be rewritten and the resultant music will also change. Your voice will be as one including all physical beings on your earth. The guttural sounds will be more melodious as you get used to this type of sound, but the transition will be swift and easy.

What will be most amazing for humanity as you go through this transition are your abilities to listen, speak to, and understand your other species. Some beings have this ability now, yet this will be commonplace in the near future.

Humanity in your world now uses hundreds of languages, many similarities from one language to another. And this is because your Earth still has many pockets of people who have come from the same planetary systems, thus language was passed down through the many generations. Since humanity's voice/sound is changing, you all will speak the same language and will be easily understood without the current language "barrier." Words used in sentences will become more sing song, more poetic. It will be most pleasing to the ear.

We salute you as you move through the energy blocks that you placed before you. The blocks are fading, and the new road or path is your choosing. Choose wisely.

May many blessings be bestowed upon each one of you.

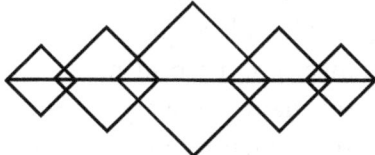

Q – What is meant by the "reversal of energy" into the form in paragraph 2?
A – The word "reversal" is our way of explaining sound through the voice. It is through this device, the voice, mimicking the frequencies activated within the body structure, an exchange of sound and light on a quantum level. Therefore to fully explain this process is not feasible here, but know that the exchange of frequencies is like putting your car into reverse. You still are moving but in another direction.

---

1   In *Mystery of the Universes* see Book 57, "Book of Celebration." The line "The song shall rise as the eagle its wings" was also written by The Oconee Native Americans who lived in the state of Nevada many years ago. These people lived in oneness with the earth. They left the earth promising that the land would once again be a haven in which they lived knowing that changes were to happen with the arrival of other "tribes."

March 12, 2010

That Gut Feeling

This, indeed, is an auspicious time, a time of great changes taking place with the incoming energetic frequencies of the dimensions most humans have never experienced. Until Now. The many changes taking place on the Earth plane are making a tantalizing entrance into a world made up of many tribes, civilizations from the many planetary systems that came to this planet of duality to experience separation at its greatest point. And that point is now diminishing, allowing for the return of the Self into the form of physicality.

    My friend, the scribe of this writing, felt the energies come into her lower gut upon asking for this writing to emerge with clarity, truth, and substance for all who read these words as well as all humanity. We always will respond with what is asked, and then so it is. Whatever you, reader, ask for is always given. Each of you is the one always in control. There is a saying in your world that says: "God is my pilot." Indeed that is true. God is always your pilot, that Self or soul that is you. Per your declaration, you made the choice to experience this level of creation to know your true Self. The veils of forgetfulness have thinned and are almost non-existent with the new levels of manifestation at hand. You are now sitting at the precipice of instant manifestation, allowing the merging of the Higher Self with this physical self called human (God man). You have volunteered to understand this level of consciousness, and you have done well. You have learned to fully integrate the emotional into the physical. Most of you understand the term "gut level," and this term is now used widely around your world. That space within your chakra system located in your 2nd – 4th chakra (sexual chakra to the heart chakra) is the location of this emotional system. Be aware of the energetic changes taking place within this center. Be aware of the deep internal feelings that emanate from this area. It is the most abstract center of the human body because of its proficiency to underlie the intellect.

This body human is quite remarkable in its ability to shake off incoherent energies that do not resonate to this emotional center. Collective humanity is now feeling this change as the higher fields of manifested energy are moving into the gut area causing some severe emotional releases. Allow these changes to take place. Breathe deeply into Self and allow the Higher Self, that God is my pilot, merge into the whole of you. Operate from this center and you will find that magnificent understandings, wisdom, will be normal operating procedure. It is the catalyst for instant manifestation in this material realm catapulting you to new levels of Self realized. From this point, life will only be grandiose, far more than you now understand or can understand. Allow this integration of love to come into your being, through this energetic portal. New doors will open unto you. You still have choice, the free will of choosing your experiences. However, those experiences shall match the new energetic blueprints of the Higher Self. It is God manifesting through you. God and You are One.

March 13, 2010

Abiding Peace

Peace as you have known it will take on a new meaning once you release the need to be in charge through the system of the ego. The ego has become such a divisive device used to manipulate yourselves into thinking that all is well when you are uncomfortable within your current system. What you see before you is the opportunity to release the programs you so carefully downloaded into your energetic systems. Those systems are now being challenged. They will not work as you move into the deeper part of your being. What is now being displayed on the outer realms is the chaos, those programs being released through the collective of humanity.

The Earth, the body of Lady Gaia, is now making her statement as she releases those programs she allowed to come into her. She now will not allow any uncomfortable low energy program disrupt her birthing process. She has made numerous attempts at dislodging these pockets of distress. And in so doing, she has made adjustments that are moving her beloved partners, humanity, to new places so she can finish her work. Dear human, please take note where her distress points are located so you can move out of the way unless you have plans to end your earthly lives. She will tarry no more as she releases these internal combustion gases to allow her to move more easily in her skin.

It is up to humanity to take in the new energy that is being propelled to Earth through the many mechanisms of this Universe. It is through the eye of the beholder, each one of mankind, to see the truths being displayed so that all will be cleansed of the ego's hold. You and Earth are being overlaid with the New Earth, a program devised by You, the collective God as One, in the form of new patterns girding the planet. As the new energies tighten their hold, humanity will have no choice but to succumb to the new matrix. The old patterns are taking their leave, not to return on this blue planet of choice. The choice is for each one of you to move the new frequencies into your physical selves, making manifestation of your life experiences take on a new form. The wonderful experiences you will enjoy are complete loving and abiding peace. The wars of years past and present are taking their leave as the ego tries to hold on, yet it cannot. The "new" energy of love shall permeate all. It is soft, it is effortless, it is unrelenting.

Humanity will lose its ability to control one another through the ego. The idea of control of one over another is that part of the ego that says that one knows better than another. This trick of the ego has gone on for many millennia, and now it takes its leave. As man allows the higher frequencies to penetrate his body, the way the body processes its life force is changing, allowing the emergence of the thought to take form through the holy scepter of the heart. Yes, the heart is the central pump of the human body, yet it takes on an increased role with its ability to discern truth. Manifestation, the way it was done in the old world through careful thought through the center of the mind is breaking away to allow the pump of life to renew the body and thoughts into the changed form. Yes, this world will vastly change as humanity gets used to manifesting through the heart. It is happening now. Have you noticed the changes going on? The physical Earth is making her releases known. You are experiencing more earthquakes, tsunamis, hurricanes, floods, winds, and these will continue until the Earth is balanced in the higher frequencies. Which means you, as humanity, have no choice but to change with her with this inpouring of higher dimensional frequencies. Also world governments are being challenged with their new agendas, some trying desperately to hold on to control even though the people are saying no. World finance is going through huge transitions and it is far from being over. This includes large corporations, how they have been managed, the products and services they have produced and plan to produce. Look at their products and services. Do they serve humanity? We understand that all products and services only serve small parts of the overall world population. But do they serve even the small sector? Those that have no respect for the people will crumble. The people, you humanity, are the ones making the decisions. As you move further into the higher dimensional life, your interests will change and they will not be tied solely to the ego. Manifestation of your wants and desires will show themselves almost immediately once the thought form has been released. Miracles will abound, or seeming miracles. It is humanity realizing their potential and their true ability of being the creators.

What you will find is the ego no longer will have the need to be fed. Truths are being told, secrets being discovered, mysteries solved. It is such a unique world you live in because you have made it so. The truth is out there, but more so, the truth is in the inner being of each and every one of you incarnate on this earth. Realize your true potential. Let it rise within your very soul. Acknowledge the love that you are made of. Speak only in gratitude, for that is where the love is felt. We take this leave to leave you with the banner of good tidings for you to hold onto, then you can loosen your grasp and let the love flow. And so it is.

March 26, 2010

Your Circumstance

It does not matter where you are in your life patterns at this auspicious time. You have been in the process of releasing all of the so-called negativity of duality lived while on this Earth plane. You now are transcending duality to live in balance of the divine feminine and the divine masculine. These two seemingly opposites are not opposites at all. They are your creation to experience, separated by you to determine what it is like to be a creator. You have had free will and will continue to have such will as you move along your paths of your created creations. What is next is up to each one of you, but as a collective, your creations will continue to be magnificent. And these creations are changing because you, as a collective, have decreed it so. And so it is.

The economy is rapidly declining in the world view, yet we say to you it is not. It is just changing to reflect your new creations. No longer will you have separate economies and monetary systems. No longer will you fearfully view your brethren on the opposite side of the earth. No longer will you entail the divisions that you have so courageously endured during the last few millenniums as being just a part of being human. It was an experiment you all have taken part in. And now you have said that is enough. And now you are seeing those divisions highlighted so you can look at what has been created by you. Not only is the earth involved, but also the other planets in your solar system as well as over 166,000 civilizations, planetary systems, and multi-worlds of form. Now you know why this is such an auspicious time. Yes, the planets are in alignment in your solar system and also the center of your galaxy, and your galaxy with The Great Central Sun. As you move closer into alignment, you get caught in a whole other matrix of possibilities. The push and pull of these alignments do have an effect on the earth as well as on your bodies. You have moved this human form to receive another form of creation that is and will be created by the collective You.

It is up to you, my brethren, to determine how you want to play within this new form. It is up to you, our friends, to determine creation as a form to adjust to or as a prototype of evolved beings using all of your capabilities to form new worlds with the blink of an eye. It is just that easy to perform, within the human body, the tendencies to manifest beauty without the hold of the old duality program. Believe it is Now that all opportunities exist within this realm. For the New Earth is locked in this matrix to enhance the well being of everyone on this planet. It is the new plan unfolding. How it unfolds is totally up to the human species. Your friends and brothers/sisters (many civilizations have no gender) of The Brotherhood of the Creative Forces are here to assist in any way that is asked of them. They are also a part of you and you soon will realize that you reside in many bodies simultaneously. The worlds of form and the formless surround you. You breathe in their essence because you are all part of All That Is.

Soon the dust of duality will clear and you will easily see what you feel you must do to create the new reality. Your focus will become clearer as you wipe away all the old patterns of creation to start anew. The difficulty of releasing can be made easier with the acknowledgement of the divine you. Once this acknowledgement is made and understood, then all thought patterns can more easily be focussed on creating with deep emotions. The human has this capability of having an emotional body which makes the transitioning more difficult, however, when you infuse the feeling of love in all you do and say, then the ability to manifest what you truly desire is that much easier. And as you continue to manifest with this gratitude, then the world will be changed in the blink of an eye.

The old world of diverse religions will eventually fade away to allow all people to rejoice within themselves as part of the One. You now are seeing changes in all religions around the world. Many will be folding within the next decade as truths are being displayed and people are waking up to the fact they have been misled due to the control of the few, and they are still trying to hold on to their power. Their grip is loosening. The pope of the Catholic religion will have many internal problems to solve and he will find that these problems cannot be solved. Soon the "flock" will disband and the disillusionment pronounced. Your current pope will soon leave his post and the cardinals will elect his replacement. However, this position will not last much longer as people will be able to see through any deceit that has gone on. The religion of Islam will grow, and then fall as more women take their power that is theirs. Any religion that promotes one race over another, or one gender over another will fall. In the new society, all will be given equal opportunity to live their own lives without the control of any one government or religion.

Humanity, now is the moment when all will be seen with new eyes. Your perceptions are rapidly changing, seeing your world anew.

Dear Reader,
I thought that this would be a good place to include my conversation with Sananda regarding questions about his life and teachings while he was incarnated as the one known as Jesus.

April 28, 2005

Conversation with Sananda

Q - Sananda, I have read many channelings/books and have had many visions regarding your life as Jeshua ben joseph and there are many differences among them all. Also I have "heard" that the life that we know as Jesus is really a compilation of three men. Please comment on this subject.

A - Greetings! You ask many questions about my life as Jesus. That lifetime was a bridge to the new light that had not been experienced on this earth for many thousands of years. It was determined that the energy in and surrounding the earth needed to change in order to fall in the divine order of our Creator.

You ask about there being a compilation of three lives of men that make up the One you know as Jesus in your Bibles. There are many accounts of that life told by my family as well as those who called themselves scribes in that day, approximately two to three thousand years ago. I came into the body of the one that is known as Jeshua, who today is known as Jesus. Yes, I was fully awake to who I was throughout that entire life. My teachings survive this very day. Also, there were six men and women who became as the "paparazzi" of that day who wrote much information about my life. They felt that they were doing a service to man by writing what they thought they saw and heard. These people were not privy to the words and love that came forth through my teachings. They thought that they understood what was being spoken but they understood not.

Therefore to answer your question regarding the three men that make up my life of Jesus is correct in that all of the writings did not adequately portray who I was thus they included other teachers and prophets of that day. Even my Mother Mary did not understand all that I was to do and what I spoke. Even her writings through others do not adequately tell the truths of my life.

My writings and teachings of those days still hold true today. Just listen in your own hearts and you too will hear the messages of Creator. My teachings may assist you but to receive the true messages of our Divine Creator is to listen within. Never did I say to worship me as a man or as a divine deity. I am divine, as is all of humanity. Those that dwell in your religions are searching for the meaning of life and they will not find it in any book. They will only find it when they acknowledge that they are divine also and live in that truth and love. You need no one to tell you what to do. Just listen, listen. Can you hear and feel the love of Creator?

Some of the testaments of long ago have been kept in safe places yet to be discovered. Some of those writings have been destroyed by man as well as through the changes of the earth.

Q - Many people travel to places where you have walked, still trying to rewrite history with the true facts of history. Could you please comment on this?

A - My dear, history is always being rewritten. History is how you view yourselves. Just acknowledging that you are divine takes you out of that constant search for a truth. When you acknowledge that you are divine, a part of God, then what other truths do you really want? You are and there is no more to it! Now to do "your Father's will" is to follow that of your heart. All of us are on a journey. We are here to co-create. You are now connecting to other parts of yourself and you are finding that you are much more than just the human body. You are a body of God. When you truly live your life knowing this, then your life will flow with ease and grace. When you know only love and joy then your are living in the state of Christ Consciousness.

My lineage continues today. *Sananda revised this text and added the next three sentences on 5-21-10.* I have family and humanity is family. Biologically, when in the incarnation of Jeshua ben joseph, I fathered three offspring, a daughter and two sons. I also fathered many other children in my other earthly lives. It does not matter who they are. They may be all who read these words. Would that knowing make a difference in your life? You each is here for a reason and that is to love and respect wholly and unconditionally your own selves. If all were to do this, then this world indeed will be the magical kingdom it was designed to be.

June 1, 2010

The following includes more questions about Sananda's lifetime as Jeshua ben Joseph or Jesus.

Q – *You have said that in the lifetime as Jesus, you had three children.*
A – Yes.

Q – *With your "balance" partner Mary Magdalene (one known with that name)?*
A – Yes. I knew her as Mariana (my lovely Mary).

Q – *Were your children born before or after the so-called crucifixion?*
A – Anna was born in my 21st year. Benjamin (pronounced Benjameen) was born in my 24th year, and James my 26th year. The crucifixion took place in my 32nd year.

Q – It has been written that you were 33 years old when sentenced and nailed on the cross.
A – I was 32.

Q – You once mentioned that during the crucifixion, the "body" on the cross was a projection of you.
A – All lives are a projection of you.

Q – Did your "projection" as Jesus succumb to death on the cross?
A – No. I did not die at that time. I, as well as my many friends and healers, knew how to maintain the body during such machiniastic doings. The lawmakers were indeed afraid of me (my abilities).

Q – Your ministry or teachings were given when your children were born and shortly thereafter. Any comment on this?
A – Yes, this was my life. I was given the many truths of life and experienced a more integrated life force, thus my abilities to transcend the third dimension. Transcending dimensions is not a miracle as such, yet appears so when viewed from the third dimension. As you know, most all humanity is transcending from the third dimension into the fourth/fifth dimensions in your present time.

Q – Thank you for your clarifications.
A – I humbly serve now as I did in that incarnation.
   Note: *The lineage of Jesus is the House of David, and the lineage of Mary is the House of Benjamin.*

April 6, 2010

The Magistrate

Time as you know it is indeed changing. It is becoming more of an afterthought than a forethought. Therefore, is it really a thought at all? Indeed, it has been a thought and because of it being a thought, it became a part of your reality. What once was, is, and what is, once was. Therefore there is no delineation from the past into the future.

Time is considered a sequence of events. And from your perspective, the past has shaped the future. And it has. However, in the course of events throughout your earthly lives, there has been a change in the frequencies of your living life and it is changing the way you see yourselves. It is changing the timeline so to speak. What once was considered the past can now be your future in that you can go back or forward to live with conscious thought and motive. Therefore you can change your story however you want. Remember you are doing this new way of living with the other parts of yourself/God and that includes collective humanity. It is in this patterning that you will see yourselves differently than you have perceived in the so-called past. You will find that you cannot change many of the specifics as to damage your new perception of life. You are living in a New World, and this New World vibrates at a higher frequency than the 3rd dimensional world. Therefore when you "go back" to another time, you will see things differently. What was perceived as events can now be looked upon as experiences caused from the collective consciousness in a more dense frequency. Many of you have heard that "everything is not as it seems." And that is because it depends upon your individual perception.

Each day is a new day. Or more correctly said, each moment is a new moment however many times you connect to that moment. Confused? Each moment is your creation caused by your thoughts going into the void and formulating the nether or god particles into a cohesive pattern, thus bringing it into your awareness of physicality. This is a simple way of explaining creation. Now where do your thoughts originate? Each one of you has the ability, and remember all is divine, to pull any pattern into your awareness, and by doing so, you combine certain attributes to your creation. What is "new" to you is your combination of various patterns already in the various matrices of creation. But where do these patterns first come from? They come from the internal voice of Creator. This patterning goes well beyond the human mind, yet the human mind is part of this overall Creator. In order for the human mind to grasp this information is to let go and let god, that part of each one of you to tap into this Collective. Your perceptions will continue changing as you start living in more parts of your Higher Self. You will see yourselves differently than you have, and you will understand the significance of the game you all have been playing. It has been a most magnificent game, and it is ending. And a new game is starting. It is you becoming more of the Collective You so your creations can be experienced in a new way.

A magistrate is a low-ranking judicial officer with limited jurisdiction. We have limited ourselves to play this game we designed. Even though we are limitless, we have limited our perceptions so we can experience our creations. Who judges us? Each of us "judges" ourselves in how we present and live within our own creations. Our identities as limited humans are being expanded as our minds/hearts expand into the unlimited Creative source of which we are all a part.

April 12, 2010

Freedom

Freedom is in your hands. It has always been this way, as humanity has always had free will. This will not change. Humanity will soon realize the diversity of his beingness, and he will then imagine the likeness created within each person. Imagination is what you create from your being. It is your image that you see and experience. You have been told through your holy script that you are made in the likeness of God Creator. And indeed you are because you now know that you are a part of God. What you have not realized, yet, are the many blocks you have put in your way so you could not see yourself for who you truly are. Therefore you have yet to feel freedom in its fullest sense.

Freedom is you taking all of your own power and using it to create the most magnificent life you can imagine. That is what God Creator intended as he breathed each of you forth for you to experience Him/Her and for Him/Her. The energy of the All is the energy of God/Prime Creator. It is in your likeness that enables you to perform on your own stage. And you have done it very well. The next stage is being set up for each one of you to imagine with more tools to work with. You will have the capacity to imagine a whole new life story. Each of your stories will intermix and whopping stories they will be. You will experience freedom like you never have experienced before as a human. There will be no need to have any of your limiting laws you have created so you can live more harmoniously with one another on your Earth. You have treated our Lady Gaia with less dignity than she deserves, but she has loved you greatly even though humanity has displayed their ignorance of the knowledge of her divine being. That ignorance is no more and shall rapidly dissipate as more of humanity wakes up to everyone's own divine essence including that of our dear Lady Gaia.

The tools we speak about are the tools that have always been available for man, yet man could not see these as he placed more blocks in his view of himself. The stage of new life is being prepared by each and every one of humankind, yet not all of humankind has to eyes to see this grand happening. The emotional freedom, a more unique part of man, coupled with the new physics as man widens his perception of creation or the ability to create with an opened Eye, will allow the new human unlimited freedom to express his ideas and desires. A new day is upon you. It is up to each and every one of you to recognize this grand force at work. Your beloved Gaia is moving to her new place in the heavens. And, you mankind, are moving with her so you can create the most magnificent life you can now imagine. Your imaginations will work with one another giving Creator a greater understanding of a new pattern of creation. You will be criss-crossing through the heavens taking in multiple creations then arranging them in a manner of new expression. This will be done with ease and wonderment.

You will be as a newborn baby awakening to a new world of endless possibilities. Your creations are in your hands working through your true heart, the light of love that passes through the All of You. Now it may be difficult to imagine such a scenario, yet as you widen your perceptions, you will see the grand adventure reaching further into the new cosmos of understanding. You will recognize the divine in All and you will use that recognition to enhance your imaginations/creations. Look within the heart of the One of which you are a part. Look at and feel the pulsations of life available in the void. The light streams through connecting all points of this life. It is up to you to use this light wisely. The mechanics of understanding are changing as you experience these pulsations. It is like taking your first steps as a toddler. You can recognize the possibilities yet not sure how to take that first step. Once you take that first step, all succeeding steps will be that much easier. You will travel to new places now in the making. You shall become the new gods, some of you having your own planets to develop. Others of you will be developing new technologies not yet seen on this Earth. But the most important part of being Creator is you knowing you are such. And so it is. A new day dawns upon Earth and humanity. See the rays of light as they stream through all Creation. You are the beloveds.

We Are One
Come, come
I hear the inner voice calling.
I speak to you about who you are.
"Who Am I?" I exclaimed.
Listen, listen intently.
Shhhhh! I hear love calling from my heart.
Your heart is my heart. Do you feel our pulse?
"I feel, I feel, I feel!" I said excitedly.
So now you know,
We are ONE.

Index

A
Adam and Eve 15
Adolphus 243, 244, 245
aerodynamics 8
aerospace 8
Airophim 104
Akashic Records 59, 61
Alchemy 152
Alcyone 147, 170, 177
Andromeda 72, 128
Anunnaki 33, 79
Anochian star 167, 171, 175, 176
Antarees 21
architecture 201
art(s) 99, 100, 155, 201 - 203
Artemis 10
ascension xii, xiii, 54, 67, 90, 106, 122, 161, 182, 199, 218, 238, 243
Ashtar 171
Atlantis 147
atom(s) 227
Avalon 80 - 82, 152, 154

B
Baal 245
Bible 79, 237
biolocation 91
biology 21, 43, 46, 55, 127, 146, 148, 162, 165, 175, 201, 203, 216
black holes 23, 24

blood 123, 162
brain 32, 95, 144, 185, 186

C
cell(s) 17, 41, 88, 122, 123, 133, 148, 149, 153, 162, 165, 220
cerebium 30, 32, 186
cetaceans 244
chakra 105, 162, 253
christ(ed) xi, 15, 21, 105, 137, 143, 262
chromosome(s) 67, 123, 178
Crea 133, 135, 138
cross currents 92
crystal(s) 29, 123, 129, 130, 131, 165, 167 - 169, 192, 201, 202
crystalline 104, 167, 192, 201
crystallized 162, 166, 172, 187, 219

D
diode(s) 30, 32, 33
DNA ix, xii, 15, 64, 70, 123, 153, 178
Dolphinian(s) 241, 242
dolphins 241, 244, 245
dream(s) 5, 15, 27, 36, 38, 47, 55, 56, 91, 101, 102, 110, 128, 139, 140, 150, 151, 155, 156, 160, 162, 173, 185, 189, 191, 193, 203, 208, 213, 235, 236

E

ego 97, 194, 199, 225, 232, 247, 254, 255, 256
Egypt 88, 147
electromagnetic 8, 9, 21, 64, 78, 92, 144, 208, 215, 239
electrons 124
Elohim 32, 104, 135, 166
endorphins 59, 61, 62
evil 15, 105

F

Flower of life 228
force field 20, 21
forgiveness 247
free will 4, 42, 159, 160, 169, 206, 248, 253, 257, 267

G

Gaia xi, xii, 1, 26, 54, 60, 65, 68, 98, 104, 107, 109, 114, 115, 127, 129, 138, 163, 171, 208, 209, 238, 239, 242, 254, 268
Galopian 168, 169, 176, 177
genes 67
genetic(s) 30, 70, 133, 140, 162, 202, 217
gods of Turan 33
Grand Plan 181
gravity 9, 171
Great Central Sun 128, 239, 258
Great Pyramid 130
Greece 147

H

Hall of Records 59, 61
heart x, xii, 10, 17, 18, 23, 33, 46, 57, 58, 64, 67, 73 - 75, 87, 88, 95, 98, 104, 105, 109, 128, 133, 134, 136, 160, 162, 174, 181, 182, 199, 200, 203, 231, 232, 235, 244, 249, 250, 253, 255, 261, 268, 269, 270
heaven 3, 4, 12, 15, 21, 28, 43, 58, 70, 72, 83, 90, 91, 109, 111, 235, 239, 243
horizon 127, 140, 214, 215, 216, 229
human genome 30, 32
hydroponics 92

I

interplanetary travel 91

J

Jesus xv, 131, 156, 157, 232, 244, 259 - 263
Jupiter 183, 184

K

karma 227, 237
King Arthur 81, 152

L

law of attraction 158, 159
ley lines 64, 65
light rays 114
lightbody 219

M

magnetic(s) 9, 59, 61, 62, 65, 202, 208, 225
Malkuth 145
Manchu tribe 76, 77, 79
manna 164, 237
matrix(es) 1, 38, 50, 55, 68, 90, 93, 95, 96, 125, 127 – 129, 150, 151, 164, 181, 186, 209, 215, 239, 255, 258
Mayans 212
Melchizidek 2
merkaba 18, 20, 23, 130, 219
metamorphosis 54, 104, 215
Michael 2, 233
Milky Way 61, 69, 212
mind x, xii, 4, 6 – 11, 15, 17, 18, 21, 22, 24, 26, 37, 41, 42, 44, 46, 51, 59, 60, 64, 67, 69, 72, 73, 78, 81, 87, 91, 108, 109, 129, 147, 167, 169, 177, 180, 197, 203, 207 – 209, 211, 227 – 230, 232, 244, 255, 266
mitochondria 146, 148, 149
monetary systems 205, 206, 257
moon(s) 18, 19, 166 – 172, 176, 211, 228, 230
music 202, 203, 250
musical 23, 203, 250

N

Native American 250, 251
Nefilim 21
nether 7 – 10, 12, 147, 265
neutron(s) 186, 187
New Age 70, 84, 108, 165, 188
nitrogen 162

O

Om 22
On 136 – 138
orbs 240
Orion 168 – 170, 176
oxygen 92, 162

P

photosynthesis 59, 62, 146, 148
photon 105
physics xv, 9, 102, 115, 139, 190, 209, 228, 268
pineal 144, 186, 219, 232
pituitary 62
Pleiades 72, 177
prana 12
pyrotechnics 146, 148

Q

quantum physics xv, 9, 115, 139
quartz 201, 202

R

Ra 134
rapture 68, 90, 91
relationships 68, 69
religion 34, 82, 259
Roman Empire 85, 88

Round Table 81, 152, 154

S
salvation 131, 135
Sananda xvii, 2, 131, 244, 259, 260, 262
silver cord 20
Sirius 72, 168 – 170, 175, 176, 244
sodium 122 – 124
sol 167, 228, 229
solar cross 142 – 144
solar plexus 17, 160, 191
sun 30, 55, 101, 127, 129 – 131, 157, 160, 166, 175, 183, 184, 214, 228, 238 – 240, 248

T
temptation(s) xi, 14, 15, 81, 231, 232
Tesla, Nikola 7, 9, 10
teutonic(s) 7, 9, 10
The Great Experiment 178, 181, 214
The Lazarus Project 21, 23, 24
Thoth 2
time travel 91, 92, 148
transchannel 91

U
UFOs 242
ultra-humanity 55
unicorn 64, 65
Uriel 2

V
vortex 23, 186

W
wavicles 209

Z
zanambiism 102, 103
Zealots 76, 77, 79

www.ingramcontent.com/pod-product-compliance
Lightning Source LLC
Chambersburg PA
CBHW070536160426
43199CB00014B/2274